PROFILES IN FAITH

50 INSPIRATIONAL READINGS BASED ON LIVES OF PEOPLE WHO CHANGED THE WORLD

HAROLD J. SALA

BARBOUR BOOKS

An Imprint of Barbour Publishing, Inc.

Published by Promise Press, an imprint of Barbour Publishing, Inc., P.O. Box 719, Uhrichsville, Ohio 44683, www.promisepress.com

Member of the
Evangelical Christian
Publishers Association

Printed in the United States of America.
5 4 3 2 1

DEDICATED TO

My grandchildren—
William, and Andrew,
Taylor, Ryan, Cole, and Carson,
Christian,
and my young friends everywhere,
who, with God's help,
will make a difference in our world.

CONTENTS

PREFACE

Following the darkness of September 11, 2001, when terrorism raised its evil and ugly head in America, a new generation of heroes was born as common men and women performed uncommon feats of valor. The attacks on the New York World Trade Center and the Pentagon in Washington, D.C., brought one of America's darkest hours, yet when we had all but thought courage was dead, tremendous feats of uncalculated risk were performed by police officers, fire fighters, flight attendants, businessmen and women, and scores of others from all walks of life, who laid down their lives to save others—heroes in every sense of the word.

Forever etched on our memories—along with the replay in our minds of the collapse of the twin towers of the World Trade Center—is the courage of those like Todd Beamer who prayed the Lord's Prayer with Lisa Jefferson, a GTE customer supervisor, then cried out, "God, help me. Jesus, help me." And asked, "Are you guys ready? Let's roll!"

No matter how deserving hundreds of men and women are who were heroes during that dark hour and the days that followed, this book goes beyond what they did, embracing the deeds of men and women who have lived down through the centuries whose lives are profiles of faith, courage, and heroism.

This book contains brief profiles of fifty of my heroes—merely a few of the men and women who are heroes and worthy of emulation. They are in a different category from the heroes of the average youth today who confuses celebrities with real heroes. This book is an outgrowth of my admiration for men and women who have made a positive difference in our world.

The men and women that you will read about are not perfect individuals at all. Each of them was completely human, flawed in certain ways, yet they all seem to possess three qualities: 1) integrity, 2) commitment to their ideals and beliefs, and

3) the willingness to stand apart from the crowd. The world could not force them into its mold, nor could it label and box them. Each was entirely his or her own person.

Harold J. Sala
Mission Viejo, California

A PURPOSE IN LIFE

DAVID LIVINGSTONE

*"And surely I am with you always,
to the very end of the age."*

MATTHEW 28:20

He left his heart in Africa, but his body is interred with the great in Westminster Abbey in London. At his death, natives gently removed his heart and buried it in the Africa he so loved. Then his body was carried to the coast, where it was shipped back to England for burial. His name: David Livingstone, born in Blantyreshire, a mill town in Scotland where he grew up.

The small flat where this great missionary doctor and explorer grew up is now a museum, and on display there are artifacts and memorabilia from his years in Africa. In a firm hand, he wrote in his diary of the devastating loneliness and pain he experienced following the death of his wife, Mary. "Oh my Mary," he wrote, "how often we wished for a quiet home since we were cast adrift in Koloburg, and now you have gone to a better home, our home in heaven."

What sustains men and women who leave behind family and comfort to go to another country for the gospel's sake, as did Livingstone? More directly, what kept Livingstone there when, as a medical doctor, he could have lived comfortably in his native Scotland?

Livingstone, himself, answered that question. After sixteen years of service in Africa, he returned to Scotland and was asked to speak at the University of Glasgow. One of his arms had been rendered useless, the result of a lion's attack. His body bore physical evidence of the suffering he had endured with twenty-seven bouts of jungle fever. His face, a leathery brown from exposure to

11

the elements, was creased from the cares of a hard life battling the Turks and the slave traders.

A hush crept over the students who listened to this man, realizing this was no ordinary person. "Shall I tell you what sustained me amidst the trials and hardships and loneliness of my exiled life?" he asked, and then he gave them the answer. "It was a promise, the promise of a gentleman of the most sacred honor; it was this promise, 'Lo, I am with you always, even unto the end of the world.'"

At Livingstone's death, they found his body bent in prayer as he knelt by his bed, beside him a small, well-worn New Testament opened to Matthew 28. In the margin beside verse 20 was this notation: "The Word of a Gentleman."

Did Livingstone feel that he had made a great sacrifice? Not in the least. He said, "People talk of the sacrifice I have made in spending so much time in Africa. Can that be called a sacrifice which is simply paying back a small part of a great debt owing to our God which we can never repay? Is that a sacrifice which brings its own best reward in healthful activity, the consciousness of doing good, peace of mind, and a bright hope of glorious destiny hereafter? Away with the word in such a view and with such a thought. It is emphatically no sacrifice. Say, rather it is a privilege."

As the body of Livingstone was carried through the streets of London on its way to its final resting place in Westminster Abbey, one man wept openly. A friend gently consoled him, asking if he had known Livingstone personally. "I weep not for Livingstone but for myself," the first man said, adding, "he lived and died for something, but I have lived for nothing."

Livingstone's life motto was, "I will place no value on anything I have or possess, except in its relationship to the kingdom of God." He lived that motto.

BOLDNESS

SIMON PETER

Peter, an apostle of Jesus Christ. . .
Grace and peace be yours in abundance.

1 PETER 1:1–2

Meet Mr. Simon Peter. Some folks call him St. Peter, and some history books use his Aramaic name and call him Cephas, but Jesus gave him the name Peter, meaning "Rock." If Jesus thought of him as being as hard or as tough as a rock, it's pretty obvious that Peter didn't wear black, have lace on his handkerchief, or sit around singing hymns all day, drinking vinegar to keep from smiling.

Peter was a pretty tough character in his younger days. Born to Jonah, a fisherman who lived in northern Galilee on the shores of the sea, Peter joined his buddies James and John and ran a fishing business that gave them a pretty fair living. Surely the wind and weather bronzed and etched his face, and the long hours of labor battling the seas and the nets hardened his muscles and strengthened his back.

Four qualities define him. First, Mr. Peter was a man of action. He never vacillated. He may not have always been right, but you knew where he stood. He did what he thought was right. It was this quality that made him a leader. Second, Peter was a man of commitment and loyalty. Once Jesus entered his life, Peter quickly walked away from his nets and vowed allegiance to the Carpenter-Messiah from Galilee. "Lord, no matter what others may do, I'll die for You!" And third, Peter was a man of courage. When the temple guards seized Jesus as He prayed alone in the garden, it was Peter who quickly drew his sword in defense. Peter denied Christ as he warmed his

13

hands outside the house of Caiaphas, but he was the only one who even tried to stay close by Jesus in His hour of trial.

The closer he was, physically, to Jesus, the more secure he was psychologically; and inversely, the farther away he was physically, the greater his insecurity and difficulty.

Simon Peter was a man of conviction. "I say You are the Son of God!" shouts Peter as he waves his fist in the air to drive home his point. That same conviction, fired by the outpouring of the Holy Spirit, caused Peter to become the leader of the early church and eventually give his life for the cause of Jesus Christ. According to tradition, Peter was crucified upside down, because he did not deem himself worthy to die as his Lord had died.

There's something of this man in us all, and the way God used him with his faults and failures gives us hope, for God is still changing people.

• • •

THE MOTHER OF THE NILE
LILLIAN TRASHER

Religion that God our Father accepts
as pure and faultless is this:
to look after orphans and widows in their distress and
to keep oneself from being polluted by the world.

JAMES 1:27

Over eight thousand orphans called her Mamma—the offspring of Muslims, Christians, and pagans—but to Lillian Trasher they were only babies who desperately needed food, clothing, a place to sleep, and as much as anything else, a mother's love.

On October 8, 1910, Lillian and her sister Jennie sailed for Egypt with no support of a mission board, and just enough money to make their way to the home of a missionary Lillian

14

had met before she left home in America.

When the sisters arrived in Egypt, Lillian, the outgoing, more aggressive younger sister with a "can-do" personality, was ready to set Egypt on fire, but she wasn't exactly sure where the matches were. Her life ministry unfolded in one of those almost larger-than-life stories where God used an ordinary person to accomplish extraordinary feats when the odds were impossibly stacked against success.

Lillian had been in Egypt for barely three months when there was a loud, disconcerting knock at the door. It was evening and no guests were expected. Lillian jumped to her feet as the door was opened. A man, half crying, spoke Arabic in staccato bursts as he explained that an Egyptian woman was dying, and he pleaded for someone to come help.

Lillian threw her coat around her shoulders as she said, "Let me go!" Reverend Dunning, the man who had invited the sisters to come work with him, was more than happy to stay behind as Lillian and two Egyptian coworkers followed the stranger.

Entering a smelly, windowless hut, their eyes slowly became accustomed to the darkness. Lying on a straw pallet was a young woman. Lillian knelt by her side. Suddenly the young mother, perhaps sixteen years of age, opened her eyes, looked into Lillian's face, and cried out, *"Arjouky, arjouky! Takhdihom!"* Moments later she died.

Then Lillian noticed a newborn baby, a tiny undernourished infant lying in the lap of an old woman. A weak, concerted cry came from the lips of the struggling infant who flailed its tiny arms. Lillian shrank back.

One of the Egyptian coworkers softly asked, "Mees Lillian, do you know what that young mother said to you before she died?" Then looking away, he said, "She wanted you to please take the baby home with you."

The old lady forcibly placed the tiny child in Lillian's arms, who, not knowing what to do, took the infant back to the missionary compound. Was this her mission in life? The circumstances all were against it. At the missionary compound, the cries of the tiny infant, badly undernourished and slowly dying, kept the rest of the missionaries awake nights. Finally the director told her, "Either you take the baby back to the village or you have to leave."

She left. With barely enough money to rent an empty house and only enough money for food that would last a week, the orphanage at Assiout, Egypt, on the banks of the Nile River, was begun.

CARING FOR OTHERS

DOUG NICHOLS

" 'Inasmuch as you did it to one of the least of these My brethren, you did it to Me.' "

MATTHEW 25:40 NKJV

Doug Nichols describes it as "what seminary can't teach." It's one of the lessons learned in the school of experience, otherwise described as "the school of hard knocks." In 1967, Doug, who today heads a Christian mission known as Action International Ministries, was serving as a missionary in India. When he contracted tuberculosis, he was eventually sent to a sanitarium to recuperate.

Though he was living on a support scale not much higher than the nationals who also were hospitalized in the government sanitarium, people thought that because he was an American, he had to be rich.

While he was hospitalized, Doug offered tracts or Gospels of John to others, but he was politely rebuffed. It was obvious that the patients wanted nothing to do with him or his God.

Discouragement set in.

Doug was often awakened in the night by the rasping sound of coughing, both his and others. Early one morning Doug noticed an old man trying to sit on the edge of the bed, but because of weakness, he would fall back. Exhausted, the old man finally lay still and sobbed. Early the next morning the scene was repeated. Then later in the morning, a stench began to permeate the ward; the old man had been trying to get to a rest room.

Says Doug, "The nurses were extremely agitated and angry because they had to clean up the mess. One of the nurses even slapped him. The man, terribly embarrassed, just curled up into a ball and wept."

The next morning—about 2:00 A.M.—Doug noticed the old man was again trying to generate enough strength to get himself out of bed. This time, though, without thinking, Doug got out of bed, went over to the old man, put one arm under his head and neck, the other under his legs, and gently carried him to the rest room. When he had finished, Doug carried him back to his bed.

The old man, speaking in a language Doug didn't understand, thanked him profusely, and then gently kissed him on the cheek.

Eventually Doug drifted off to an uneasy sleep. In the morning he awakened to a steaming cup of tea served to him by another patient who spoke no English. After the patient served the tea, he made motions indicating that he wanted one of Doug's tracts.

"Throughout the day," says Doug, "people came to me, asking for the Gospel booklets. This included the nurses, the hospital interns, the doctors, until everyone in the hospital had a tract, booklet, or Gospel of John. Over the next few days," he added, "several indicated they trusted Christ as Savior as a result of reading the Good News!"

The world doesn't care how much you have or what you know; they want to know how much you care.

CHARACTER

MRS. NOAH

The world was not worthy of them.

HEBREWS 11:38

She is the mother of everyone you will ever meet, yet we don't know her name. We know only that she lived during a period of world calamity and distress—unlike anything the world had ever known before or since. We also know that she supported her husband and became a woman who rightfully takes her place in the annals of world history.

In the Bible, she is identified only as "the wife of Noah." For someone who was so very important, very little has been written about "Mrs. Noah."

Today, all the people of the world can trace their lineage to this woman. When you look at the record carefully, it's easy to see what a great woman she was and how much she contributed to the history of humanity. Mrs. Noah is a woman whose true worth has never been recognized.

Perhaps these snapshots of Mrs. Noah will help illustrate her true value and worth.

First, picture Mrs. Noah, the wife of an unpopular preacher. Behind almost every successful man there is a woman, and few ever consider what it must have been to live with a man who was the mockery of his day. Think how discouraged Noah must have been facing the hostile men and women who laughed at him when he pronounced the coming judgment of God. Mrs. Noah knew the heartache that comes to preachers' wives today when there is failure. After the flood, Mrs. Noah suffered the heartache of seeing her husband struggle with alcohol, yet she stood by her husband and worked through their problems.

Next, picture Mrs. Noah as the mother of three sons who grew up playing with the children of those whose values were much different than hers and her husband's. Mrs. Noah did a good job with her boys. Surely Mother Noah had to wipe tears from her boys' eyes when their friends mocked them because of their father's strange ideas.

Now picture Mrs. Noah as a grandmother. All children want their grandmothers to tell them bedtime stories, but none who has ever lived could rival the stories Mrs. Noah told when innocent grandchildren asked, "Grandma, tell us a story!" What vivid, eyewitness accounts of the flood those grandchildren must have heard!

Mrs. Noah was all of the above, plus a great deal more. Surely she must have been included in those of whom the writer of Hebrews wrote, "The world was not worthy of them. . ." (Hebrews 11:38).

COMMITMENT

MOTHER TERESA

"The King will reply, 'I tell you the truth,
whatever you did for one
of the least of these brothers of mine, you did for me.'"

MATTHEW 25:40

She was born in what is now known as Macedonia, just north of Greece. Her parents were constantly hounded by poverty. Her father died when she was seven years old, and her mother was forced to start a business selling embroidered cloth. Her brother, determined to make something of his life, became an army officer, and when his sister, at the age of eighteen, decided to give her life in missionary service, he chided her, "Why don't you make something of your life!"

Defiantly she hurled back the words, "You think you are so important as an officer, serving a king of two million subjects. Well, I am serving the King of the whole world."[i]

In 1976, the brother stood in the company of admirers in Stockholm as his sister—the one who he first thought was wasting her life—received the Nobel Prize for her work with the poor.[ii]

The brother was known as Lt. Bojaxhui. The sister will be remembered affectionately as Mother Teresa. When the frail figure who won the hearts of the world died of cardiac arrest at the age of eighty-seven, the world mourned.

Dynamos come in small packages, and this woman less than five feet in stature, created a tremendous explosion of care and compassion for the outcasts and suffering of the world.

At her death accolades came pouring in from both the rich and famous and the poor and insignificant. "The saint of the gutters," "a living saint," "the hero of the poor," "angel of mercy," and a host of other titles was bestowed on this little woman who hobnobbed with the great and mighty but never varied from her absolute commitment to the poor and destitute of the world. While some may differ with her theology, none can fault what she did.

A few paragraphs are insufficient to describe the qualities of this great woman who is a hero's hero. She was her own person who never hesitated to rebuke those who disagreed with her, yet she wept with the suffering and dying. When the situation demanded it, she was as tough as nails.

Mother Teresa had many admirable qualities—humility, compassion, loyalty, love for the suffering and outcasts, even a keen sense of humor. Most important was her unswerving commitment to God's calling, no matter how difficult, no matter how great the personal cost, or how lowly the task to which she felt God had directed her. When she ministered to the poor, she thought of it as ministry to Jesus Christ. A colleague who knew her well said, "She didn't look at masses of people. She looked at. . .one face, one smile, one heart, one person at a time."

She told her biographer Chawla, "We are called upon not to be successful, but to be faithful."[iii] And faithful she was. Her last words were, "Jesus, I love You. Jesus, I love You." It was this that drove her and kept her pressing on.

At Mother Teresa's death, India's president K. R. Naryanan, said, "Such a one as she rarely walks upon this earth."

When she died, her light was not extinguished. By the time of her death, more than four thousand sisters had joined her, ministering in orphanages, homes for the poor, AIDS hospices, and centers for the poor and destitute. They will carry on the work she began.

• • •

BYRD BRUNEMEIER

I am not ashamed, because I know whom I have believed,
and am convinced that he is able to guard
what I have entrusted to him for that day.

2 TIMOTHY 1:12

On the wall of our Guidelines' studio is a rusty .30 caliber rifle shell mounted on a wooden base. It is a rather strange artifact to adorn the wall of a Christian recording center, but a story lies behind it.

It was one of the thousands of shells and implements of warfare gleaned when engineers on the island of Saipan cleared a site for the installation of the Far East Broadcasting Company's powerful radio station. The rifle shell was found at the base of "suicide hill," where thousands of Japanese soldiers had flung themselves to their deaths when it seemed that capture by the Allied Forces was imminent. On that death site has risen a tremendous antennae field that will broadcast the message of life to men and women throughout Southeast Asia.

No one has done more to convert the scene of tragedy to a field of victory than Byrd Brunemeier, a quiet, unassuming engineer who spent most of his life as a missionary—much of it in missionary radio. Byrd was never one to waste words, but when he said something, people listened. Byrd had the patience to sit down with kids and explain the difference between transistors and vacuum tubes—but he also had the knowledge to put together superpower stations that reached around the world.

Byrd was tough, resilient, and committed. He was totally dedicated to the cause of Jesus Christ, whom he served with reckless abandon. When equipment had to be procured, instead of spending mission funds, Byrd would scour the alleys and electronic junkyards of Manila for parts and then put something together far superior to anything that could be bought.

On July 22, 1983, Byrd made radio contact with his wife, Angie, who had been sent to the United States for surgery. He had just finished cleaning up the field under the shortwave antenna and was preparing to fine-tune the powerful KSAI transmitter. Finishing the contact, Byrd said, "Good-bye until next Friday."

By Friday, however, Byrd's body lay in a simple grave in the Protestant cemetery on Saipan. Here is what happened: while he was adjusting the equipment, a fire broke out in the transmitter. Racing to hit the power cutoff, Byrd stumbled and fell into a high voltage power line. As Angie put it, "He fell into the arms of his Savior."

"For the child of God there are no 'accidents'—only 'incidents,'" wrote someone long ago. That had to be true of Byrd.

His wife, Angie, wrote, "Time after time Byrd was near death, or just barely missed being killed. It is because of this that I have the assurance that his death at this time was no accident. It was our Father's perfect plan."

···

LIM CHEONG

And my God will meet all your needs
according to his glorious riches in Christ Jesus.

PHILIPPIANS 4:19

When Lim Cheong bought a three-bedroom house with two bathrooms and moved into it, it represented far more to him than the mere pleasure of owning his own home. For him, it represented a kind of spiritual victory as well.

You see, Lim Cheong's father, a silversmith, earned his living by making silver gods and selling them to the people who came to the local temple in Cambodia. Lim Cheong thought about the gods that his father made, and he began thinking about what they could do, or could not do. He knew that people prayed to them, but he wondered, "Were those prayers answered?"

At the age of twelve, Lim Cheong went to his uncle, a Buddhist priest, and asked if he knew of a prayer that had ever been answered. The uncle admitted that he was uncertain. Not satisfied, Lim Cheong went to a missionary and asked the same question. Without hesitation, the missionary related numerous incidents in which God definitely answered prayer; the missionary went on to tell Lim Cheong about God's love in Christ Jesus. Lim Cheong decided to serve the God who is alive and answers prayer.

That evening, he told his father what he had done. The father shouted, "Get out of my house. Go sleep with your Jesus!" Then Lim Cheong had to put his newly found God to the test. Would God take care of him? What does a twelve-year-old boy do who has been thrown out of his own home?

God did take care of him. After graduating from Prince Sihanouk High School, Lim Cheong received a full university scholarship but turned it down, feeling that God was calling him into Christian service. After he completed his education at a Bible college, Lim Cheong married and became a pastor to his people in Cambodia.

Then in 1964, foreign missionaries were asked to leave the country. Fearlessly, Lim Cheong still carried on God's work. He was imprisoned in a test case that resulted in his release.

Eventually, one by one, his entire family embraced Jesus Christ as their personal Lord and Savior.

Today Lim Cheong is a pastor and broadcasts God's love to his fellow citizens. He can no longer shepherd them directly, for the religious freedom that Cambodia once enjoyed has been lost. But the God who took care of a twelve-year-old boy and proved His care for him is just the same as ever.

CONVERSION

AUGUSTINE

I am not ashamed of the gospel,
because it is the power of God
for the salvation of everyone who believes:
first for the Jew, then for the Gentile.

ROMANS 1:16

Amidst the crumbling ruins of the Roman Empire in the year A.D. 354, one of the greatest champions of Christian faith was born in a small North African province. His name was Augustine.

As a youth, Augustine was reared in the church of his day, though at first the church seemed to make no great impression on him. His mother was a Christian; his father was a noble Roman. In his late teen years, Augustine, like many young men and women today, turned to philosophy, and under its influence he turned from the church. His heart was seeking for an answer to the questions of life. At first he thought he found peace in a pagan religion called Manicheanism, but soon Augustine was seized with doubt and agnosticism. For a period of time, he drifted and doubted, still seeking anchors for his restless heart.

In his autobiography that bears the title *Confessions*, Augustine tells about this period of great turmoil and unrest. He indicates that he shared in the vices and corruptions of his day. For a number of years he lived a double life of immorality. Then in the year 387, Augustine found faith in God through Jesus Christ His Son. Augustine's seeking heart found an answer that has satisfied the restlessness of people in all ages.

In spite of the life that he lived before he found Christian faith, Augustine made one of the greatest contributions to Christianity that has been made since the time of the apostle Paul. He is one of the few men in history who is equally loved and respected by Catholics and Protestants alike.

Augustine experienced the depths of sin, yet he found that the grace of God is greater than the greatest sin. Augustine's approach to Christian faith began with his assertion that the human heart is entirely corrupted by sin, which he defined as "choosing our own way rather than God's way." He said there is nothing in the heart of human beings that is worthy of God and that all we could ever do would never bring us to a place where we could be worthy of the Savior.

Augustine held that only by the grace of God could anyone find eternal life. And he was right, for the apostle Paul said, "By grace are you saved through faith, and that not of yourselves, it is the gift of God; not of works lest any man should boast." Augustine's life was really no different than the lives of countless thousands today—seeking, restless, drifting. In his *Confessions*, Augustine wrote, "Thou has made us for Thyself, O God, and our heart is restless until it finds its rest in Thee."

...

PAUL

Christ will be exalted in my body,
whether by life or by death.
For to me, to live is Christ and to die is gain.

PHILIPPIANS 1:20–21

Some are born great; some have greatness thrust upon them; and some could be dumped out of an airplane over a foreign country and achieve greatness. These are the truly great. Such was the individual born long ago of Jewish parents in the university town of Tarsus, located in the Zagros Mountains of Turkey. During the first part of his life, he was identified as Saul of Tarsus, but following a dramatic encounter with the risen Christ, he became known as Paul the Apostle.

No other individual so shaped and molded the future of Christianity as did this scholarly and dedicated individual. As an author he contributed thirteen books to the New Testament, writing more books than any other person and second only to Luke in volume. As the theologian of the first century, he settled doctrinal issues, set in order rules for church government, and became the missionary who spread the Good News through the known world, from Jerusalem to Rome and perhaps as far west as Spain.

Following his conversion, which you can read about in the ninth chapter of the book of Acts, Saul, as he was then known, went on to Damascus, where he recovered his sight following the blindness that had occurred as he traveled to Damascus. His conversion was immediate and complete. Whereas he had been the greatest enemy of Christianity, he now became its great proponent and evangelist, traversing seas and continents in the relentless pursuit of converts.

Following his conversion, Paul met with much skepticism

from the Christian community, something that was to be expected. After three years in exile in Arabia, he returned to Damascus and then to Jerusalem to meet with Peter and James, the Lord's brother, who had become a leader in the church. He then went back to his hometown in Tarsus and made tents until, about seven years later, Barnabas sought him out and said, "Brother Saul, the Lord has need of you!"

Paul and his traveling companions made three extensive missionary journeys and, in the process, planted the flag of Christianity in many a town and city. He was often abused and imprisoned for his faith. Writing to the Corinthians, he opened his heart, saying, "We are hard pressed on every side, but not crushed; perplexed, but not in despair; persecuted, but not abandoned; struck down, but not destroyed" (2 Corinthians 4:8–9). He also received the traditional thirty-nine lashes from his enemies on five occasions. Three times he was beaten with rods, once stoned.

Tradition says that Paul sustained two long periods of prison, once for almost two years under house arrest in Rome, where he wrote letters to the churches, and then a final imprisonment about A.D. 67, when he was martyred. Paul's goal: "Christ will be exalted in my body, whether by life or by death. For to me, to live is Christ and to die is gain" (Philippians 1:20–21).

CONVICTIONS

MARTIN LUTHER

For it is by grace you have been saved, through faith—
and this not from yourselves, it is the gift of God—
not by works, so that no one can boast.

EPHESIANS 2:8–9

While October 31 is Halloween to many people, to others it marks the anniversary of the day a German priest, outraged by abuses he saw in the Roman Catholic Church, nailed a document to the door of the cathedral in Wittenburg, Germany. Known as the *Ninety-five Theses*, Martin Luther's document created an uproar unlike anything that had troubled the church for centuries—perhaps ever. Before his death in 1546, this man was responsible for dividing the church, establishing the Protestant Church, inaugurating the Reformation, translating the Bible into German, and introducing the Christmas tree into the nativity observance.

The son of a Saxon miner, Luther was born at Eisleben on November 10, 1483. At the age of eighteen, he entered the University of Erfurt, where he studied prelaw. Then in the summer of 1505, Luther was caught in a thunderstorm that threatened his life. So thankful was he that he escaped unharmed, he vowed to become a monk. True to his promise, he entered the Augustinian monastery at Erfurt and was ordained in 1507. Eventually Luther received a doctorate in theology and was appointed as a professor of Scripture—a position he held for the rest of his life.

On a visit to Rome in 1510, on business for his Order, Luther was shocked at the practice of buying and selling indulgences. Today we think of an indulgence as when we have a second or third piece of dessert. However, in Luther's day, as a kind of prepayment for sins the buyer had not yet committed, indulgences (thought to bring God's forgiveness) were sold in the streets to pay for the construction of massive St. Peter's Cathedral in Rome.

This angered Luther, and an angry Luther troubled the conscience of the Middle Ages church that had compromised the Scriptures. Luther never intended to split the church of his day; he simply sought to bring them back to the historic position held by the apostles and the early church fathers.

Visitors to Rome today can still view the Church of the Scala Sancta, or the Church of the Sacred Steps—thought to have been the ones Jesus walked up as He approached Pilate's judgment hall and later moved to Rome. As Luther was crawling up these steps, kissing each one, the impact of what he had been studying came crashing down upon him: "The just shall live by faith" (Romans 1:17 KJV). Luther's keen mind struggled with the issue of how sinful man finds forgiveness: By what he does as good deeds? Or by what Jesus did when He died on the cross? The impact of what Paul wrote—"the just shall live by faith"—finally caused Luther to cry out, "Fide sola!" (Faith alone!) And the Reformation was born.

Scripture led Luther to evaluate the practices of his day, and the Word of God alone became the foundation of Luther's teaching and preaching. Paul's letters played a prominent part in Luther's theology. He stood against anything he felt was in defiance of God's Word.

Martin Luther—the man who changed the church, which changed the world!

COURAGE

ATHANASIUS

"Are you then the Son of God?" He replied, ". . .I am."

LUKE 22:70

It can fairly be said that in the history of Christendom, never has so much been owed to one man as is owed to a pugnacious, argumentative preacher by the name of Athanasius. Frankly, if Athanasius were alive today, it is likely we wouldn't much care for him. Folks didn't then, either.

Athanasius was born in Alexandria, Egypt, about A.D. 297. When he was five years old, Diocletian, the Roman emperor, proclaimed himself to be a god and demanded to be worshiped. When Athanasius was eighteen, Constantine became the emperor, and things began to change fast.

Athanasius was tough, everybody agreed. He used words like a street fighter uses left jabs. Exiled five times in forty-five years, he should have gotten the message, "To get along, you've got to go along." Not Athanasius. He stood by his convictions when friends and supporters abandoned him.

To appreciate what we owe this man, you must understand the issues. Athanasius believed the Bible taught that Jesus Christ was very God of the very God. In other words, He did not become God when He was born. He always was God. He believed that Jesus Christ laid aside His exercise of authority as God, or His attributes of deity, as theologians describe it, and became man. But he was no ordinary man, believed Athanasius. He was the unique fusion of man and God.

Others disagreed. Led by Arius, who was Athanasius's archenemy, others taught that Jesus became God, the highest of all created beings. In the last 150 years, some groups have adopted Arius's teaching, which makes Jesus merely a good man who rose to the same spiritual heights as we can today.

With the overview of history, church historian Bruce Shelley says that if Athanasius had gone along with the crowd, "It would have meant that Christianity had degenerated to a form of paganism. The Christian faith would have had two gods and a Jesus who was neither God nor man. It would have meant that God Himself was unapproachable and totally removed from man. The result would have been a Christianity like a host of pagan religions."[iv]

The one teaching that separates Christianity from Judaism, and more recently from the teaching of cult groups, is the truth that God exists as one in three persons: Father, Son, and Holy Spirit. Yet, contended the pugnacious Athanasius, there is one God, not three.

If Arius had won, Christianity would have been just another

religion, and Jesus Christ would have been a great teacher but nothing more. If Jesus Christ was God, as Athanasius contended, then He demands our allegiance and our worship. One man against the world was eventually vindicated by the truth, and for that we owe Athanasius a great debt of gratitude.

• • •

"PONGO"

"In the same way, any of you who does not give up everything he has cannot be my disciple."

LUKE 14:33

Ernest Hemingway once said that "courage is fear that has prayed!" If he's right, then a Zamboanga man has that kind of stuff. (Zamboanga is one of the principal cities in Mindanao, southern Philippines, an area torn by strife in recent years.)

"Pongo" is his nickname, and he's a radio engineer with the Far East Broadcasting Company. He was there the day that Muslim gunmen drove a motorcycle into the FEBC compound, ran into the studio, and with guns spewing deadly bullets, shot and killed Greg Bacabis, the FEBC engineer who kept the station running, as well as Greg Hapalla, a pastor whose gospel program was aired over the stations.

That was enough for Pongo. He knew that he might very well be the next person to be gunned down. He had a wife and children, and he didn't want to take the risk.

Pongo had a motorized pedicab—a motorcycle with a sidecar attached, which is used for inexpensive transportation. Pongo reasoned that he might be able to turn the sideline into a real moneymaking business, at least enough to support his family. The risk of being killed in traffic was less than being shot by a terrorist.

In the days that followed, however, as Pongo drove his pedicab, he thought of the two men who had died for the cause of Jesus Christ, and he began to understand how the disciples felt when they all fled as Jesus was arrested in the garden.

"Enough!" Pongo finally thought. He went back to the radio studio and told the staff that he would be ashamed to die in a traffic accident. If he had to be killed, he wanted to die for the cause of Christ.

He went about his work quietly, apprehensively. He prayed and waited. Then it happened. In the words of a colleague, "A few days after Pongo returned to work, a motorcycle raced into the studio compound. Remembering that the gunmen had come in on a motorcycle before, the staff feared they had returned to finish the job of killing all the broadcasters. People dove under tables and desks. . .hid behind cabinets. . .scrambled to get into closets.

"But not Pongo. He deliberately walked to the console in the studio and sat down. 'If I'm to be shot,' he said, 'I'd rather be broadcasting the gospel—not hiding under a table!' "

It was a false alarm and nobody was hurt, but Pongo didn't know that when he walked into the studio and took his place at the controls. The real heroes of the faith are the unknown, unnamed men and women who are willing to lay down their lives for what they believe.

• • •

WILLIAM CAREY

*By faith he [Abraham] made his home
in the promised land like a stranger in a foreign country. . . .
For he was looking forward to the city with foundations,
whose architect and builder is God.*

HEBREWS 11:9–10

When Chuck Wickman polled some fifteen hundred youthful Christians and asked them, "Who was William Carey?" he was in for the shock of his life. How many could identify Carey? Not one, yet William Carey has appropriately been called the "Father of Modern Missions," and his book on missions, written in 1792, so stirred the Christian world that it ranks alongside Martin Luther's *Ninety-five Theses* in its influence and consequences.

Born to a poverty-stricken family in 1761, near Northampton, England, William Carey suffered from allergies that kept him from pursuing his goal of becoming a gardener. At the age of sixteen, he was apprenticed to a shoemaker; shortly thereafter he was converted to faith in Jesus Christ.

A lack of formal education didn't stop this determined young man who set out to change the world. Of Carey, Warren Wiersbe wrote, "By the time he was in his teens, he could read the Bible in six languages. He later became Professor of Oriental Languages at Fort William College in Calcutta, and his press at Serampore provided Scriptures in over forty languages and dialects for more than 300 million people."

Never was there a more unlikely candidate for success than this young man, who at the age of nineteen married the sister-in-law of the man to whom he was apprenticed. Following his now famous sermon to a group of ministers where he uttered his well-known quote, "Expect great things from God; attempt great things for God," he volunteered to go to India as a missionary.

At first Carey's wife, Dorothy, adamantly refused to go. His father considered his going to India an act of absolute madness. Meanwhile, the shoemaker to whom he was apprenticed died, and Carey assumed the financial responsibility for his widow. Boarding a ship for India with his eight-year-old son, Carey was turned back before the ship left England. When he finally boarded another ship, his wife reluctantly relented and joined him on the journey to India. She knew she would never be happy, and she wasn't. Her health and disposition both deteriorated. She constantly belittled Carey, urging him to quit and take the family back to England.

Carey, rebuffed by the East India Company, sought work in an Indian factory and spent evenings each week translating Scripture or preaching. The tragic death of their son, little eight-year-old Peter, caused Dorothy's mind to snap, and she never regained her mental equilibrium. Until her death in 1807, Dorothy never shared her husband's desire to make Christ known. Yet Carey struggled and endured in the face of failure. For seven long years among the Bengali people Carey had grown to love, he could not claim a single convert.

If ever a man had cause to relent and give up, it was William Carey. In 1812 a warehouse fire destroyed his two grammar books, his massive polyglot dictionary, and whole versions of the Bible that he had translated, yet Carey knelt, thanked God that he had strength, and started the task all over again.

Carey died in 1834 but not before he left an indelible mark on his beloved India and, more than that, on the mentality of missions around the world.

• • •

PETER TEN BOOM

Let us not become weary in doing good,
for at the proper time
we will reap a harvest if we do not give up.

GALATIANS 6:9

The name of his famous aunt, Corrie ten Boom, is still widely known in Christian circles, while few have heard of her nephew. Yet Peter ten Boom felt just as strongly about saving the Jews as did Aunt Corrie (*Tante Corrie* as Peter called him, using the Dutch word for "aunt"). The ten Boom house, a short train ride from Amsterdam, became a safe house to which Jewish people could escape from the Nazis.

When Dutch patriots learned that the SS troops were systematically raiding the orphanages and taking Jewish children, then sending them to their deaths in the concentration camps of Europe, brave Dutch men would impersonate SS officers at the risk of their lives, raid the orphanages, and take the Jewish babies to the ten Boom house, until they could be sent to safe houses and farms where people adopted them as their own.

Only God knows how many children were saved, but their numbers were in the hundreds before the Germans finally raided the family home and sent the ten Booms to prison.

Peter ten Boom was a committed Christian first and a Dutch patriot second. During the German occupation, Peter served as an organist in a country church, playing the pipe organ for services. Though it was forbidden by decree of the Germans, on one occasion Peter pulled out the stops of the organ and at full crescendo played the Dutch national anthem, while shocked but proud churchgoers stood to their feet and sang the words. For this act of defiance, Peter, then age sixteen, went to prison.

After the war, Peter went throughout the world with the same message as his famous aunt: Forgiveness is the only answer to hatred that never dies.

Peter was in Israel on a speaking tour and had a heart attack. Going home was out of the question. Immediate surgery would be the only thing that could save his life. As the cardiologist chatted with Peter before the operation, he said, "I see your name is ten Boom. Hmm. Are you by any chance related to the ten Booms of Holland?"

"Yes," replied Peter. "That is my family."

The doctor replied, "And I am one of the babies your family saved!"

The doctor then saved the life of Peter ten Boom and paid back a debt in full.

• • •

Wang Ming Dao

I have finished the race, I have kept the faith.
Now there is in store for me the crown of righteousness.

2 Timothy 4:7–8

On July 30, 1991, life in Shanghai, China, was pretty normal. Ships and water ferries moved up and down the Huangpu River; streets were crowded, and it was business as usual. On that morning, a small group of men and women quietly slipped into a tiny, one-bedroom apartment in Shanghai to blend their voices and prayers in a memorial service for ninety-one-year-old Wang Ming Dao. Actually, the service had been scheduled for the following day, but fearing that far too many people would come, having learned that this godly old saint had slipped into the presence of the Lord, family and friends decided to go ahead with a private memorial service on Tuesday instead of the scheduled Wednesday.

Wang Ming Dao was one of the most influential Chinese Christians to have lived in this century, and while some might think it strange that only a small private memorial service was observed in the small, one-bedroom apartment where Wang and his saintly wife lived, things aren't done in Shanghai the same way they are done elsewhere.

In China there is a lot more to think about than flowers and special music. Wang Ming Dao was also an ex-convict, having once been sentenced to death row under China's penal code. When visitors from outside would visit the little apartment where the Wangs lived, they would discreetly close the blinds to hide their presence from prying eyes.

The Communist government charged and convicted him of being a "counter revolutionary" and sent him to forced labor in the northern part of China, where he worked in a prison coal mine for twenty-two years and nine months. His real crime was that Wang was committed to Jesus Christ. When the Communists closed the churches in the early 1950s, Wang defiantly said, "They can close our churches, but they cannot stop us from worshiping God in the confines of our homes!"

I met Wang and his wife for the first time when he was eighty-nine. He was hard of hearing and almost blind, yet he was alert; and in spite of everything he had been through, he had retained his sense of humor. In 1981, following his release from prison, Wang wrote an autobiography called *A Stone Made Smooth*. When I said that I had read his book, he replied with a twinkle in his eye, "Stone still not yet smooth!"

Wang Ming Dao is part of the reason that the church inside China is among the fastest growing in the world despite the repression by a government committed to atheism.

Shortly before his death, when asked what lesson he could share with the church elsewhere, he firmly and resolutely replied, "Tell them to walk the hard road!" Wang Ming Dao was one of the greatest of all time. And at the end of the hard road, he met his Master, Jesus Christ.

DETERMINATION

RAY BUKER

I have fought the good fight, I have finished the race,
I have kept the faith.

2 TIMOTHY 4:7

In the Olympics of 1924—the one in which the Scotsman Eric Liddell took two gold medals—another, little-known athlete medaled as well. His name: Raymond Bates Buker. While Eric Liddell eventually went to China as a missionary, Ray Buker served in Burma, on the China border. Though Buker couldn't recall meeting the Flying Scot who distinguished himself because he refused to run on Sunday, the two would have liked each other.

Both were champions; both chose to champion a cause greater than winning in the Olympics, the cause of proclaiming the gospel of Jesus Christ.

Meeting Dr. Ray Buker left quite an impression on me. I was a young seminarian, not especially interested in world missions. Unlike most seminary professors who come to class dressed in something like a brown tweed sport coat with baggy trousers, Ray Buker walked into the classroom dressed in the garb of a Burmese male. As students watched, somewhat mystified, Buker climbed onto the top of his desk and sat cross-legged for the rest of the hour, teaching his class without moving. Don't think that didn't impress us.

In his biography *Against the Clock,* Eric Fife says that by the time Ray and Dorothy Buker arrived in Burma in 1926, there were already two hundred American Baptist missionaries there, whose lifestyle was anything but hard, which wasn't what Buker had in mind.

He asked to be sent to a difficult place. He explained that he was an athlete and was disciplined, accustomed to hardship, and willing to go to places other people couldn't handle. It was that spirit that brought him north into China, where he established a mission station and planted the cross.

In 1942, the Bukers, continuing to serve though World War II had begun, narrowly escaped death, fleeing before the advancing Japanese army. Joining the ranks of the newly formed Conservative Baptist Foreign Mission Society, Buker was asked to head the work, which, for the next ten years, became the fastest growing mission society in the world.

The last time I saw Ray Buker, we lunched together near the retirement village where he lived. Instead of finding a rocking chair, Buker had measured out the distance in the halls that would allow him to jog a mile or two each day. He was in his late eighties.

When Ray Buker died at the age of ninety-two, he left behind a rich legacy scattered throughout the world, for through his life hundreds of men and women gained a vision of a world that needs the undiluted gospel of Jesus Christ. Ray Buker, Olympic athlete and missionary statesman without equal.

DEVOTION

BROTHER LAWRENCE

Whatever your hand finds to do,
do it with all your might.

ECCLESIASTES 9:10

Few people in the world can honestly say that God disappointed them, yet Nicholas Herman was one of them. He was converted to Christianity at the age of eighteen. Seeing a dry, lifeless tree in the dead of winter and realizing that soon it would burst forth into life as the sap rose in the spring, Herman knew that he was spiritually dead and asked God to give him a rebirth. It happened, too; for a period of time, Nicholas Herman served as a footman and a soldier.

In 1666, Nicholas Herman was admitted to a lay brotherhood at the Carmelite monastery in Paris. Herman entered the order expecting to suffer at the hand of God because of his prior sinful life, but God disappointed him. Instead of a life of regret and suffering, Herman, who was given the name of Brother Lawrence, found forgiveness, joy, and peace beyond expectation.

Brother Lawrence's faith, however, was soon put to the test, for he was assigned to the kitchen. By nature, he was awkward and clumsy. Kitchen duty was a challenge, but the way that he tackled it provides guidelines for victorious living three centuries later.

Lawrence believed that even the most mundane and worldly task can be done in love for God, and doing it for the great King gives the most humble task a spiritual purpose. In his little book *The Practice of the Presence of God,* Brother Lawrence shares what God taught him. He wrote, "The time of business does not with me differ from the time of prayer, and in the noise and clatter of my kitchen while several persons are at the same time calling for different things, I possess God in as great tranquility as if I were upon my knees. . . ."

He wrote that he began each task with fervent prayer and then did it with love for God. At the end of the meal, he prayed again with thanksgiving. Lawrence wrote, "We ought not to be weary of doing little things for the love of God, who regards not the greatness of the work, but the love with which it is performed."

To Brother Lawrence the practical aspects of Christianity could be summed up in three words from the pen of the apostle Paul: faith, hope, love. He said, "That all things are possible to him who believes, that they are less difficult to him who hopes; that they are more easy to him who loves, and still more easy to him who perseveres in the practice of these three virtues." Putting faith, hope, and love into operation was to Brother Lawrence practicing the presence of God. What a legacy!

EXCELLENCE

W. PAGE PITT

I can do everything God asks me to with the help of Christ who gives me the strength and power.

PHILIPPIANS 4:13 TLB

W. Page Pitt is a man who should have failed, but he succeeded. For years, Professor Pitt headed the Department of Journalism at Marshall University. Although he was offered salaries of two to three times what he made as a college professor, Pitt's first love was teaching journalism.

Pitt's success is enviable because of the record he has made, but what is most remarkable about Professor Pitt is that he accomplished all of this practically blind. When he was only five years old, he lost 97 percent of his eyesight. Though almost blind, Pitt refused to attend a school for the blind and was accepted in public school. He played baseball, first base, catching a low ball by the sound of it whistling through the grass. He played football as a second-string tackle. He worked his way through college and graduate school, inveigling his fellow students to read his lessons to him. When he became a professor, Page Pitt earned the reputation of being a "slave driver." But he also earned the reputation of being a topnotch professor. They did not come any better than Pitt.

One day, a somewhat thoughtless student asked the professor which he would consider the worst handicap: blindness or deafness, or no arms and legs, or what? "There was a smoldering, ominous quiet," says his wife. Then Page exploded. "None of those things! Lethargy, irresponsibility, lack of ambition or desire: They are the real handicaps. If I do not teach you anything but to want to do something with your lives, this course will be a magnificent success!"

No one could challenge Pitt. Constantly he would growl at his students, "You're not here to learn mediocrities, you're here to learn to excel." Pitt would often tell his students, "If I send you out on a story and you cannot get it because you have broken a leg, call me before the ambulance comes and I'll forgive you. But do not give me excuses! They wound me, and explanations pour salt in the wound."

Pitt is right. The real enemies we face, the ones that deal us the most severe blows are not the handicaps of blindness or deafness. There are enemies far worse: lethargy, irresponsibility, lack of ambition, and lack of desire.

Exploits
for God

Billy Graham

Woe to me if I do not preach the gospel!

1 Corinthians 9:16

Billy Graham has preached the gospel to more people than any person in all history. In the flyleaf of his autobiography *Just As I Am*, the publisher notes the following: "Billy Graham Crusades have reached more than 200 million people in person, and millions more have heard him on radio, television, and film. He has been welcomed behind the Iron Curtain, into China and North Korea, and on every continent."

Billy has often said, "The first thing I am going to do when I get to heaven is to ask, 'Why me, Lord? Why did You choose a farm boy from North Carolina to preach to so many people. . . ?' "

If the greatest ability in the sight of God is availability, that may be part of the answer. Sherwood Eliot Wirt, the founding editor of Billy's *Decision* magazine, a man who worked closely with Billy Graham for nearly forty years, came to know him very well. He says, "All attempts to explain Billy Graham fail unless they begin at the cross."

William Franklin Graham II grew up just outside of Charlotte, North Carolina, and was raised by hardworking, nononsense parents who attended the local Presbyterian church.

When Billy was a teenager, a group of Christian businessmen held an all-day prayer meeting in the Graham family pasture. At that prayer meeting, businessman Vernon Patterson prayed that "out of Charlotte the Lord would raise up someone to preach the gospel to the ends of the earth."[vi] Little did Billy realize that he would be the answer to this man's prayer.

By high school, Billy went to church with his family "grudgingly, or of necessity," according to his own confession; but in 1934 a controversial Southern Baptist evangelist came to Charlotte: Dr. Mordecai Fowler Ham. When Ham publicly denounced the morality of some of the students in Billy's high school and the students decided to go break up the meeting, Billy determined to go just to see what would happen.

What happened is that the Holy Spirit began to convict Billy, who was converted after attending several times. He soon felt that God had called him to preach.

Billy was courted by the liberals who liked him as a man but would have preferred that he tone down his message and avoid the "conversion" emphasis. He was enticed by politicians who promised undeliverable rewards if he would throw his weight behind them. He resisted using his popularity to gain personal wealth (he continues to live on a relatively small salary set by the Billy Graham Association and has donated vast sums of book royalties to Christian work). He has been viciously attacked by his detractors, yet he answered them with kindness, even thanking them for pointing out his flaws, which he freely admitted and sought to correct. His moral life has been flawless, and his organization has been free of financial scandal.

Never will there be another Billy Graham!

FAITH

C. S. LEWIS

"If anyone chooses to do God's will,
he will find out whether my
teaching comes from God or whether I speak on my own."

JOHN 7:17

When C. S. Lewis died on November 22, 1963, most newspapers never mentioned that fact. Some papers carried a brief news note on an inside page stating that the Cambridge Professor of Medieval Literature had died of heart and kidney failure. On page one of newspapers, on the day Lewis died, was the vivid picture of an American president, John F. Kennedy, who had been cut down by an assassin's bullets.

His full name was Clive Staples Lewis, which may account for his using only the initials "C. S.," or simply "Jack" to his personal friends. Lewis was a brilliant man and a keen thinker. He wrote on a vast number of themes, including English literature, theology, and children's stories such as the *Narnia Chronicles,* filled with mythical beings and fairy tale characters.

Some refer to Lewis as an apologist, or one who defends Christianity, yet Lewis never really intended to defend anything. Nevertheless, his book *Mere Christianity,* which came from a series of radio lectures during World War II, was the tool that brought Chuck Colson to an understanding of Jesus Christ, and the book has spoken to the hearts of millions of other people. Lewis's logical, intuitive mind simply concluded that it is more rational to accept the gospel and its implications than to disbelieve it.

Lewis never based his salvation on feelings or emotional experiences. To the contrary, he later wrote that before he was converted, there were times when Christianity seemed very logical; and after his conversion, there were times when atheism also seemed logical. He believed that you have to tell your emotions where to get off, otherwise you dither back and forth, uncertain of who you are or what you believe.

His personal life was complex, and his path to faith was marked by intense struggles and personal conflicts. He never learned to drive a car, and he was a failure when it came to practical things like fixing something around the house. Though book royalties eventually amounted to large sums, he generously gave most of it away and never could handle money. But he was a master at handling words. When it came to making complex things simple, he was good—very, very good.

Lewis eventually married an American writer who admired him, and he became a father to her two children. At first, Lewis had admired Joy Gresham but didn't really love her. Forced with either the choice of marrying her or losing her because the British government was going to deport her, he married. Eventually he fell in love with Joy, and she became an inseparable part of his life.

When she died of cancer, Lewis was shattered. He felt as though God had let him down. "I turned to God now that I really need him," said Lewis, "and what do I find? A door slammed in my face, the sound of bolting and double-bolting, and after that. . .silence."

Yet Lewis held on to his faith, based not on his feelings of pain and loss, but the truth of the gospel, which rises above sensations or feelings.

• • •

DAVID

"For when David had served God's purpose in his own generation, he fell asleep."

ACTS 13:36

I often close interviews by asking, "At the end of your life, how would you like to be remembered?" The answer reveals a lot about the person.

A thousand years after King David lived, Luke, one of the writers of the New Testament, included a few thoughts about how David was remembered. He wrote, "For when David had served God's purpose in his own generation, he fell asleep. . . ." (Acts 13:36). Another translation adds a single phrase that injects even more meaning. It reads, "For when David had served God's purpose in his own generation *according to the will of God,* he fell asleep" (Nestle's Greek text, italics added for emphasis by the author).

For a moment, measure your life against the benchmark of what Luke wrote about David. Would you say that you are accomplishing God's purpose for your life? Or would you have to say that you fall far short?

Tell me what your heart yearns to do, what you think about when you're unable to sleep at night, and I'll tell you what kind of a person you really are. If money consumes your thinking, you are materialistic. If you think only of revenge, you're angry and bitter. If your thoughts are of God and how you can serve Him, you are a person of spiritual sensitivity and dedication.

What is God's purpose for your life? Good question! The Bible explains very clearly what God's purpose is for your life in simple, easy-to-understand language.

David served God's purpose according to the will of God. The writers of Scripture contend that what happens to your life is of great importance to our heavenly Father. Paul wrote, "Be very careful, then, how you live—not as unwise but as wise, making the most of every opportunity, because the days are evil. Therefore do not be foolish, but understand what the Lord's will is" (Ephesians 5:15–17). There you have it—a life of purpose, touching our generation according to the will of God!

• • •

CHANG SHEN

"The King will reply, 'I tell you the truth,
whatever you did for one
of the least of these brothers of mine, you did for me.'"

MATTHEW 25:40

The truly great saints of the world are the army of unknown, unclaimed, undecorated little people, the ones who live their lives in obscurity, unrecognized, and undiscovered. Such was a Chinese brother martyred in the backlash against foreigners known as the Boxer Rebellion in the year 1900.

If Rosalind Goforth, a Presbyterian missionary living in Manchuria, had not written about this man, we would never have known what a saint he really was. Chang Shen was poorly educated, and he had a violent temper. Until his conversion in 1886, his death would have been little noticed. At the time today's story begins, Chang was blind, thirty-six years of age, a despised, hard-drinking, violent man who cared for little but himself.

When Blind Chang, as he was called, heard that foreign doctors, who reportedly could cure blindness, were living 120 miles to the south of his home in Manchuria, he set out on the long journey by himself. On the way, the helpless blind man was beaten and robbed, and by the time he finally got to the hospital, he was forlorn, dirty, and wretched. He arrived, only to be told that there were no beds at the hospital and he would have to go away.

He had no place to "go away" to, so he curled up in the entrance and fell asleep. The night watchman had seen it all—poverty and hunger, beggars and the destitute; but when he saw this man, his heart was deeply touched. He went to Dr. Christie,

47

the chief of the hospital, and volunteered to let Blind Chang sleep in his own bed.

For a month Chang stayed at the hospital and recovered some sight, only to lose it after his release, when a local Chinese practitioner pierced the pupil of his eye with a needle, thinking that this would heal the man. Now Chang was completely blind. At the hospital, however, Chang had heard the gospel and realized he was a sinner. He was soundly converted.

When he asked to be baptized, James Webster, the missionary in charge, felt that he just wasn't ready and promised to come visit him at his home in due time. Disappointed, Chang took some tracts and a few papers about Christianity and made his way back to his hometown, where he began evangelizing. But Chang had a past, a black one as locals described it. Who would believe him?

When Webster finally got there, he found a small but thriving group of believers, all of whom wanted to be baptized. A church had been born, one that had come to an understanding of Jesus through the changed life of this blind man.

In the year 1900, the hatred of outsiders turned the tide of public opinion, and the persecution of Christians grew, especially foreigners: the Boxer Rebellion. When Christians were imprisoned, Chang agreed to give himself up to free them. Leaders of the Rebellion thought if they killed the Christians' leader, they would put an end to the growth of Christianity; on July 22, 1900, Chang was driven through the streets in a cart used to transport animals. As he went to his place of execution, he sang a song we usually think of as a children's song: "Jesus loves me, this I know, for the Bible tells me so." As he cried out, "Heavenly Father, receive my spirit," the executioner's sword severed his neck. And Blind Chang received his sight as God's child in heaven.

ABRAHAM

Trust in the LORD with all your heart,
And lean not on your own understanding;
In all your ways acknowledge Him,
And He shall direct your paths.

PROVERBS 3:5–6 NKJV

Risk your money on dice and they call that gambling; risk your money on the stock market and they call that business. But risk your future on God, and they call you a fool. Such was the way it was with a man by the name of Abraham who lived long ago.

In the event you don't remember Abraham, he holds the unique distinction of being loved and esteemed by devotees of three faiths—Jews, Moslems, and Christians. Long ago, Abraham lived in Ur, a land known today as Ancient Mesopotamia. When God began to speak to Abraham about leaving his hometown, people thought of him as a fool. Hebrews 11:8 speaks of his step of faith saying, "By faith Abraham, when called to go to a place he would later receive as his inheritance, obeyed and went, even though he did not know where he was going" (Hebrews 11:8).

Ur was a nice place. Good schools and hospitals; good stores; comfortable homes. Abraham left this all behind as he set his sights on an invisible goal.

Can you imagine some of the conversations that must have taken place as neighbors said, "We see you are packing up your family, Abraham. Where are you headed?" And Abraham says, "I'm not sure; I just know that God is leading me." "Uh-huh," comments a friend. "How are you going to take care of your family?" Abraham shuffles his feet and says, "I don't know, but

I am sure God will take care of us!"

Men and women today who live and walk by faith, like Abraham of old, will always be considered to be out of step with their peers, a kind of fanatic who takes the truth of God's Word literally. Such have always been in a minority.

Those who have heard the call of God on their lives should not expect contemporaries to understand what they are doing; the voice of God is a still, quiet one, often drowned out by ambition and greed and the desire to be in control. The life of faith has always been contrary to the logic of the world, yet obedience to the plan and purpose of God does not require that you have a full knowledge of the game plan; it only demands that you have confidence in Him who does know the plan.

• • •

J. HUDSON TAYLOR

"My food," said Jesus,
"is to do the will of him who sent me
and to finish his work."

JOHN 4:34

Among the British, Yorkshiremen are known to be tough. They are a "no-nonsense" breed of individuals known for common sense, thrift, and hard work. Understanding J. Hudson Taylor's Yorkshire background may explain why this man quietly impacted China in the last century as no other foreigner ever has done. Yet none is harder to figure out than Hudson Taylor, which may be precisely why he is so important.

Striving to answer the question "What made him tick?" is difficult. In many respects, he was very ordinary—a quiet, soft-spoken, compassionate, yet tough individual without dynamic leadership skills or outstanding physical charisma. Yet he was a man great in faith and prayer, great in commitment, and indefatigable when it came to impacting the country he adopted and loved.

Before he was born in 1832, his parents had prayed, "Dear God, if You should give us a son, grant that he may work for You in China."[vii] Some twelve years later, the young Hudson declared, "When I am a man I mean to be a missionary and go to China!" Biographer J. C. Pollock says that in spite of the fact that his father had prayed for his son to go to China, he thought the idea merely amusing that a boy as sickly as Hudson would ever go abroad.

God used that Yorkshire stubbornness to do what others with greater education, culture, refinements, and social standing never accomplished. Converted at the age of seventeen, Taylor immediately began his preparation for missionary service. Finally going to China, he labored for six years in Shanghai and Ningpo with mixed success.

Recognizing that the culture was a barrier, Taylor cut off his hair and wove a braid into the remaining locks, then dyed his scalp—something very painful since the container of lye he was using exploded, leaving facial burns—and began dressing in Chinese fashion.[viii]

Still feeling unaccepted, Taylor returned to Britain and established his own mission—the China Inland Mission—and returned in 1866 with his first group of missionaries, who were committed to reaching China no matter what the cost.

When trouble came, Taylor always sought refuge in the Lord he loved. Trusting Him implicitly for their needs—whether it was finances or missionaries to help reap the harvest—he depended on the Lord. "God's work done God's way will never lack God's supply," he used to tell his comrades.

In June 1900, an imperial decree from Peking ordered the death of all foreigners, a grim chapter of Chinese history that resulted in the deaths of 153 missionaries and 53 children, the majority of whom were connected with Taylor's mission.

He never fully recovered from this great loss, yet he planted the cross of Jesus Christ firmly in Chinese soil. It not only survived the Boxer Rebellion but also the assault of Communism a half century later.

FAITHFUL TO YOUR CALLING

JEREMIAH

"The harvest is past, the summer has ended, and we are not saved."

JEREMIAH 8:20

Before his death in 1984, Francis Schaeffer developed what some have called a "theology of disagreement." Schaeffer never abandoned his position that the true mark of a Christian is the ability to love unconditionally, yet he was also convinced that one cannot really love without hating the opposite of what one loves.

Schaeffer was not the first to articulate a "theology of disagreement." He was largely indebted to a man who lived some twenty-seven hundred years before and who made a "theology of disagreement" a science. His name was Jeremiah—a sensitive, caring individual intent on doing the will of God no matter what it cost him.

Jeremiah was almost always on the unpopular side of issues because that's where God was. Jeremiah spoke fluently, boldly, and without consideration of who would be displeased at what he said.

Jeremiah was called by God to be a spokesman, calling God's people back to Himself. And when they refused to budge,

Jeremiah told them the price they had to pay. He became a hated, despised individual, persecuted and belittled. He was thrown into prison, put in stocks, even thrown in a slime pit or a tar pit and left to die. But a foreigner, an Ethiopian, rescued him by putting rotten rags under his armpits and using ropes to pull him from the clutches of death (see Jeremiah 38).

It is no wonder that his name has become a byword for someone who is pessimistic and discouraged. There is one thing you must never forget. The God who told Jeremiah not to fear because He was with him makes that same promise to His child who has the courage to denounce wrong when truth is on the scaffolds.

FOCUS

PAUL

"I was thoroughly trained in the law of our fathers and was just as zealous for God as any of you are today."

ACTS 22:3

Imagine a friend is describing someone as "a man of middling size, and his hair was scanty, and his legs were a little crooked, and his knees were far apart; he had large eyes, and his eyebrows met, and his nose was somewhat long."[ix] Would you be impressed? Probably not, yet the description is the only one in history with any credibility that tells us what the apostle Paul looked like.

No wonder his critics said, "His letters are weighty and forceful, but in person he is unimpressive and his speaking amounts to nothing" (2 Corinthians 10:10). He was the greatest convert Christ's gospel ever produced. He was the theologian-missionary of the New Testament, and he traveled thousands of miles, often by foot, preaching that Christ died for our sins, He was buried, and He rose again the third day.

Paul was of the tribe of Benjamin, a Roman citizen by birth in the university and cultural center of central Asia Minor, Tarsus. He had studied with Gamaliel and was zealous in his commitment to Judaism (see Philippians 3:5). His first encounter with believers in Jesus Christ was in Jerusalem, as he held the coats of those who stoned Stephen.

Shortly after that came the defining moment of his life. He was on his way to the city of Damascus, intending to arrest and harass believers, when Jesus Christ revealed Himself to him. His life was forever changed. No longer was he Saul of Tarsus, but Paul, the Apostle of Jesus Christ.

Three great missionary journeys took him throughout the Roman Empire, and almost everywhere Paul preached, he established a church. Then, as he moved on to another place, he wrote letters back, thus giving us the thirteen books in the New Testament that provide us so many insights into the heart of this great man.

One of the warmest and most personal letters of Paul is his letter to believers in Philippi (the book of Philippians). In this, Paul, I believe, revealed the source of his faith and the secret of his life. Here's what he said: "One thing I do: Forgetting what is behind and straining toward what is ahead, I press on toward the goal to win the prize for which God has called me heavenward in Christ Jesus" (Philippians 3:13–14). In three words, he revealed the secret of his life: concentration, forgetfulness, and anticipation.

Concentration: No person can really succeed apart from being completely focused. In the realm of the spiritual, concentration is important, as well. Jesus said, " 'No one can serve two masters. Either he will hate the one and love the other, or he will be devoted to the one and despise the other' " (Matthew 6:24).

Then Paul mentions a wise forgetfulness of the past. Forget

your failures; they only hurt you. Your victories are history. Your losses will cripple you.

His third secret was anticipation, looking ahead. Paul put it graphically as he wrote that he was "straining toward what is ahead." He was using the imagery of his day, comparing life to a race and the world to a vast arena where athletes vied for the prize. There was no thought of turning back for Paul, of settling for less than his best effort. He was committed. He had burned the bridges behind him. There was but one way to go—God's way.

INTEGRITY

JOSEPH JACOBSON

Like a bad tooth or a lame foot
is reliance on the unfaithful in times of trouble.

PROVERBS 25:19

If you had been falsely accused of a sex crime and had been thrown in prison with no real hope for release and you could have three wishes, what would you ask for? I suspect you would ask for: 1) your freedom, 2) your identity as a person, as opposed to being a number in a penal system, and 3) revenge on the person who framed you and sent you to prison unjustly.

It happened to a man whose story is stranger than fiction. His name: Joe Jacobson. Well, that's not exactly how his name was listed on the roll of Pharaoh's prison in Egypt long ago. His name was actually Joseph, and he was the son of Jacob.

The rest is exactly the truth. Here's the record: "Now Joseph was well-built and handsome, and after a while his master's wife took notice of Joseph and said, 'Come to bed with me!' But he refused. . ." (Genesis 39:6–8). When he continued to refuse her advances, in anger she accused him of rape, and Joseph was framed and sent to prison.

Lots of people are forced into situations not of their choosing, nor of their liking, that either make or break us. How we cope with them depends on how we view them.

Joseph could have said, "God, is this what I get for trying to do the right thing?" If he ever thought of it, he never voiced it.

Joseph learned some hard lessons while waiting for God to vindicate him. For one, he learned that you can't count on friends to help get you where you want to go. When the cup-bearer found his freedom, assisted by Joseph, he promptly forgot his old friend; but Joseph learned he could count on God.

Joseph was eventually released and became the prime minister over Egypt, which would never have happened had he not been where he lost his freedom. Later, Joseph told his brothers, "You intended to harm me, but God intended it for good to accomplish what is now being done, the saving of many lives" (Genesis 50:20).

Can we be sure that God is with us? Jesus said, "Never will I leave you; never will I forsake you" (Hebrews 13:5). With that assurance, we can face anything, and win. Of that, you can be sure!

LONELINESS

AUNTIE WANG

"Never will I leave you; never will I forsake you."

HEBREWS 13:5

It is said that behind every great man is a great woman. Unquestionably, that was true of Wang Ming Dao. The woman, Deborah Wang, a frail but vibrant saint, endured what no woman should ever have to face. Her husband, Wang Ming Dao, was one of the unofficial architects of the house church movement in China. When her husband was sentenced to prison for what the Chinese government termed "antirevolutionary" activities, his wife followed. For twenty years, this saintly woman was in a separate prison, facing the bitter cold of northern Chinese winters with thin clothes and insufficient food, but she never complained.

In 1989, I sat in their humble little apartment in Shanghai, listening to them recount their experiences. I was drawn to the strength of this saintly woman whose smile came from her heart. As she talked about the years of imprisonment, I asked, "Did you ever lose hope?" (After all, twenty years of separation from the one you loved so deeply, with little news and few letters, is a long time.) Her eyes spoke far more than her answer as she said, "No, never!"

After the Wangs were released from prison, their home became a refuge for those who needed encouragement and counsel. God only knows how many cups of tea Auntie Wang (as her friends called her) served to weary men and women who traipsed up the stairs to their flat for encouragement and help.

Two weeks after her husband passed away at the age of ninety-one, I again visited Deborah Wang. "Auntie Wang," I said, "I will pray that you will not be lonely."

Pausing for just a moment, she spoke with a clear and resolute tone of voice, "I will not be lonely; I was not lonely before." I knew she had seen her husband only three times during their twenty years of imprisonment. That one word, "before," said so much.

In the early hours of April 18, 1992, Deborah Wang entered into the presence of the Lord, where a faithful and devoted husband awaited her.

She wasn't surrounded by friends and flowers when the

angel escorted her across the threshold of death. While she was alone, she was not lonely. She had the promise of her Lord, who said, "And surely I am with you always. . ." (Matthew 28:20).

OBEDIENCE

AMY CARMICHAEL

Charm is deceptive, and beauty is fleeting;
but a woman who fears the LORD is to be praised.

PROVERBS 31:30

Amy Carmichael was a woman who didn't fit the mold, which resulted in lots of problems for people who were more committed to order and tradition than to the teaching of God's Word. I highly recommend Elisabeth Elliot's book about Amy Carmichael, *A Chance to Die*. A former missionary herself, Elliot candidly and accurately portrays the humanity and charity of one of the greatest of all missionaries in modern history.

Born on December 16, 1867, on the north coast of Ireland, Amy Carmichael was never destined to mediocrity. While other children were given peppermint candies to pass away time in the long church services, the Carmichael children were expected to sit in quiet obedience.

In the early years of her missionary experience, Amy seemed to flounder. She first served in Japan, then China, then Ceylon, then back to England, where no small amount of pressure was put on her to stay home. Finally God sent her to India, and there she spent the rest of her life.

Among the many things that Amy Carmichael will be remembered for is her work among the children, especially the girls who were forced into temple prostitution. She became part of the work that had been established at Dohnavur, a name that eventually became synonymous with what she did.

If the greatness and complexity of this woman *could* be captured in three words, they would be: 1) obedience, 2) loyalty, and 3) tenderness. She had a fierce, unswerving obedience to the Word of God and what she felt was God's will for her life, something traditional missionaries neither understood nor appreciated.

Out of obedience to the will of God came loyalty to those with whom she worked. She refused to speak against her critics and would not allow her coworkers to do so, either. She insisted on absolute, unflagging loyalty to her brothers and sisters in Christ, no matter how they appeared to be enemies of the work.

In her book *Roots*, she wrote, "It is not at all that we think that ours is the only way of living, but we are sure that it is the way meant for us. . . ." She did not believe that you could pray with someone or for someone and then speak harshly of them. And in the dining room of the missionary home of Dohnavur hung a sign that read, "May the absent one always be safe at our table!"

Finally, tenderness marked this great woman's life, but not the kind of tenderness often associated with weakness. Hers was more like an iron fist in a velvet glove. She would wade through a hostile crowd of shouting, angry people to rescue a little girl from temple prostitution yet weep openly with the child over the pain and hurt she had sustained.

At the age of eighty-four, on January 18, 1951, Amy Carmichael slipped into the presence of the Lord after a long illness. Under a tamarind tree, in a grave marked only by the Indian word for mother, AMMAI, lie the remains of a woman who was as much a saint as any woman who ever lived.

OPTIMISM

BILL EATON

Unless the LORD builds the house, its builders labor in vain.

PSALM 127:1

Most people called it "an absolute disaster!" But Bill Eaton called it an "adventure!" It all started following several weeks of drenching rain, when California appeared to have had an Asian monsoon. The rains finally softened the earth, and a massive hole began to swallow up Bill and Lee Eaton's four-bedroom house, their family home for twenty-three years. Here their family grew up. Scores of good memories were made there.

Then a wrecking crew punched several massive holes in the roof before they discovered they were tearing down the wrong house.

Yet Bill says, "It's not a disaster; it's an adventure!" And how does Lee feel? "It looks ominous to me right now," she said, "but it's not an impossible situation."

How do people stay so positive when insurance won't cover the loss and they are not exactly rich? Bill and Lee Eaton are not the average sort of people. They have an optimism born of faith.

Naturally, Bill and Lee weren't exactly joyful when a city building inspector condemned their house as unsafe. They had to pick up what they could and gingerly move out, careful not to make too much noise or create too much stress for the rickety house. They could feel the house moving under their feet as they packed.

Not everyone handles trouble like the Eatons, but Bill and Lee have something going for them some folks don't have—a positive faith in God that affects their value system. They realize some things are more important than just a house.

OVERCOMING

NEHEMIAH

"The God of heaven will give us success."

NEHEMIAH 2:20

Nehemiah was a man with a mission. He had papers from King Artaxerxes of Persia that would allow him to build the wall surrounding Jerusalem. Sounds like a nice project, right? Put in a garden and get someone to plant flowers! Everybody would be happy, right? Dead wrong!

Nehemiah knew it wouldn't be easy. When he arrived in Jerusalem, he told no one of his intentions. Why? He knew that opposition would immediately mount. Finally, he brought together the leadership and gave it to them straight. He described the disgrace and dangers that resulted from having no wall around the city, and they responded (like babes without knowledge), "Let us rise and build!"

No sooner had Nehemiah begun the project when he was faced with severe antagonism. Local political adversaries tried to stop them. As the work progressed, the opposition tried scorn and ridicule. " 'What they are building—if even a fox climbed up on it, he would break down their wall of stones!' " (Nehemiah 4:3).

When the wall was nearly half built, the enemies mobilized and began to attack them. Undaunted, Nehemiah instructed that half the people should stand guard while half worked on the wall.

Trouble broke out among those who were building, as some of the folks took advantage of their brethren by charging them high prices. The rich got richer and the poor got poorer, but in all of this Nehemiah didn't quit or give in to weariness.

When the chief antagonists of the project realized their resistance was failing, they invited Nehemiah to a peace conference. Nehemiah realized this was a trick and that they actually sought to kill him. Four times he declined their invitations.

Today, Nehemiah would surely tell us, "I learned that God will honor His Word, and that it is no sin to grow tired or weary; the sin comes when you yield and compromise your conviction. I learned that the greatest enemies are not those outside the walls. They are the ones within, which we experienced when we yielded to what we knew was wrong."

When challenged and confronted with danger, Nehemiah prayed and kept doing what he knew was right.

• • •

FRED WHITEMAN

Why then be downcast?
Why be discouraged and sad?
Hope in God!

PSALM 42:5 TLB

When I asked Fred Whiteman how old he was, he replied, "I'm forty-seven on the outside and thirty-one on the inside. I've had more trouble than most senior citizens, and I still look at life through the eye of a child." What kind of an answer was that? Fred had seen forty-seven birthdays. Within his chest cavity beat the heart of a man thirty-one years old—the result of having had a heart transplant.

Within a six-month period of time, Fred lost his best friend, who died with cancer of the liver, his mother died, and his wife died in what most would term a "freak accident." Fred's heart failed him; and even then, following a heart transplant, Fred himself faced surgery for cancer, as well as being sued by the bank where his wife worked. Fred may well have some advice for Job himself.

You get the feeling that Fred has nothing to fear from life because he has faced its bitter challenge and found the strength that comes from the God who helped him meet the challenge.

He quotes Bob Harrington, who said, "When we can't figure it out, we have to faith it out." Unlike some who face times of difficulty and have nothing to fall back on, Fred is a committed believer in Jesus Christ and has spent most of his life serving the Lord.

"I never had a moment," says Fred, "when there was no hope!"

Fred doesn't understand why one man should have so many difficulties, but he isn't spending time trying to solve that question. He says that difficulty does several things for a person: 1) It gives you a knowledge of yourself that also makes you aware of your intense need for God. It makes you fully understand your humanity and the fact that we live one heartbeat away from eternity. 2) Difficulty produces character in your life and refines the integrity of the heart. It strips you of the desire to play games and pretend to be what you are not. 3) And it allows God to use you as a witness to other people, showing them that at the point of our deep need, God can and does meet His children.

He knows that firsthand.

•••

JOHN MARK

"Come, follow me," Jesus said,
"and I will make you fishers of men."

MARK 1:17

If the life of any person ever demonstrated that success is never final and failure is never fatal, it was a man who lived in Jerusalem in the first century. His name was John Mark, often referred to as just Mark. We are introduced to him when a prayer meeting was held in his mother's home in Jerusalem. And on that occasion he met a man who was to leave a deep impression on his life, Peter, who had just miraculously been released from prison. (See Acts 12.)

About the same time persecution arose under Nero, Paul took Mark along with his cousin Barnabas and started his first missionary journey. But things didn't go well. John Mark quit and came home.

When it came time for the next journey, Paul wouldn't allow Mark to join him and Barnabas; so the two cousins dropped out, and Barnabas took Mark and went to Cyprus.

After the Cyprus experience, Mark returned and spent time with Peter, whose style deeply impressed this young man so much that Mark eventually wrote the manuscript we know as the second Gospel in our Bibles today—the Gospel of Mark.

Do you see how failure doesn't have to be fatal? The New Testament contains four books often referred to as Gospels—Matthew, Mark, Luke, and John. But in reality there is but one gospel recorded by four different men with different viewpoints.

The shortest is the one Mark wrote, just sixteen chapters. Sometimes called, "the businessman's Gospel," it is fast-moving, almost staccato-like, a series of encounters with Jesus Christ joined together by a Greek word, *euthus*, which means "straightway," "immediately," or "right away."

Mark reflects the worldview of his travels and seems to write from a Roman viewpoint. He pictures Christ as a servant whose birth is unimportant. Whereas Matthew and Luke devote quite a bit of narrative to the birth of Jesus Christ, Mark skips the event entirely and immediately begins to describe the deeds of Jesus Christ. Some fourteen times he refers to Him as "the Son of man."

The foreword to the Gospel of Mark in one study Bible says, "Matthew and Luke present what might be described as a series of colored slides, while Mark's Gospel is like a motion picture of the life of Jesus." Mark wrote about selected events in the life of Jesus Christ, so that all might know the servant who became the Savior of the world.

Looking beyond what Mark wrote, we see the heart of a man deeply dedicated and committed to the cause of Jesus Christ. He emphasizes the importance of commitment and decisive action, possibly acknowledging his own failure in his early years.

Sixteen action-filled chapters give you a new appreciation for the Servant-Savior Mark wrote about.

• • •

D. L. MOODY

I sought the LORD, and he answered me.

PSALM 34:4

This book would be incomplete if I did not include a man who had a great heart for God, who radically challenged two continents for God and laid the foundation of a multifaceted Christian ministry that has encompassed the world and continues to grow even stronger with the passing of time.

Dwight Lyman Moody was a hero in his day. I've chosen this little-known incident in the life of this great man to demonstrate that heroes are normal people who struggle with the same emotions and feelings we all have. They simply are not overcome by them.

A century ago, Moody was as well known as Billy Graham is today. All over the world English-speaking people had been affected by this forceful, energetic evangelist.

In the fall of 1892, Moody boarded a ship from Southampton headed toward New York. Three days into the journey, disaster struck. In his memoirs, Moody told how he was lying on his bunk, reflecting on his good fortune, and how he had never been involved in an "accident of a serious nature." At the very moment he was thinking about it, Moody was startled by a loud noise, and the vessel began to shudder as though it had been "driven on a rock."

It was serious, very serious. The large shaft that drove the propeller had broken and smashed through the side of the ship. Water began pouring in, and soon it became apparent that the ship would sink.[x]

D. L. Moody was no stranger to dangerous situations. In the American Civil War, he had been shot at, but the bullets missed him. He was in Chicago during the great cholera epidemic and went with doctors to visit the sick and dying, but the sickness spared him. Moody said, "I remember a case of smallpox where the sufferer's condition was beyond description, yet I went to the bedside of that poor sufferer again and again. . . . In all this I had no fear of death. But on the sinking ship it was different. It was the darkest hour of my life."[xi]

Moody had never before known the cold, gnawing reality of fear. By his own testimony, "I had thought myself superior to the fear of death," but that illusion quickly vanished. "I could not endure it," he said. Moody went to his cabin and on his knees poured out his heart to God in prayer. What happened? Moody said, "God heard my cry and enabled me to say, from the depths of my soul, 'Thy will be done!' "

Moody had gotten through to God, and his fear left him. He went to bed and fell asleep almost immediately. At three in the morning, Moody's son awakened him with the good news that a steamer had heard their distress signals, and seven days later, they were towed into safe harbor.

"The darkest hour of my life" was the way Moody described it. This was a man who had preached to hundreds of thousands. In his day he spoke to more people than any man alive. He had never before experienced real fear.

No one is immune from the dark hours of the soul when fear gnaws at your innermost being. Even heroes who are spiritual giants are susceptible to the weaknesses of the flesh. James said, "Elijah was a man just like us" (James 5:17).

Scores of men and women can testify to the fact that at the darkest hour of their life, God broke through, giving them peace and courage to say, as did Moody, "Thy will be done!"

PERSEVERANCE

ANACLETO LACANILAO

*The first thing Andrew did was
to find his brother Simon and tell him,
"We have found the Messiah" (that is, the Christ).
And he brought him to Jesus.*

JOHN 1:41–42

Charles Spurgeon once said, "By perseverance, the snail reached the ark!" I don't know whether an unknown missionary laboring in the Philippines a generation ago ever heard that, but no doubt he believed it. Laboring in a Catholic country where, a generation ago, Protestant missionaries were not always appreciated, he began to tell Anacleto Lacanilao that he needed to be born again and have a personal relationship with Jesus Christ. Lacanilao, who was the father of eight children, didn't buy this new concept and shrugged off the witness of his friend, who wasn't rebuffed but just kept coming back.

On the eleventh visit, Lacanilao told the unwelcome visitor, "If you come back one more time, I'm going to kill you!" It was not an idle threat. What happened? The man came back the twelfth time! And that was when Dad Lacanilao became a believer in Jesus Christ. He later said, "When he came back the twelfth time, I figured there must be something to this experience he was talking about, and I had better listen to him!"

Today, he and his wife are both in heaven, but their eight children are all serving the Lord, some as outstanding Christian leaders in the Philippines and the United States. One of the sons is Mike Lacanilao, former president of FEBIAS College of the Bible and head of Back to the Bible Ministries in the Philippines. Another served as head of Youth For Christ; but all of the eight children followed in the footsteps of Mom and Dad Lacanilao. It all happened because a faithful witness, whose name is unknown to me, didn't stop when he faced opposition.

How quickly most of us give up when a colleague or a friend whom we have been talking to about Jesus Christ begins to give us a cold shoulder. Quickly we think, "Religion is a personal matter—he has his and I have mine!" Nothing causes enemies quicker than talking about religion or politics, right? At least, that's what we often tend to think.

If Jesus came to provide a way to heaven and there is no other way you can get there, you'd better be concerned about your neighbor or friend, your husband or wife, or the person you work with.

You have an influence that I do not have, that your pastor doesn't have, that Billy Graham doesn't have. You rub shoulders with men and women daily, and you, as a believer, are the only one who represents Jesus Christ to them. If you have talked to someone, and your witness has been rejected, remember the man who led Anacleto Lacanilao to the Lord.

PRAGMATIC

THOMAS

Thomas said to him,
"Lord, we don't know where you are going,
so how can we know the way?" Jesus answered,
"I am the way and the truth and the life."

JOHN 14:5–6

Tradition characterizes him as being strong-willed, stubborn, and doubting. His name: Thomas, one of the Twelve who walked with Jesus. Mentioned a dozen different places in the New Testament, Thomas is usually thought of as a "show me" sort of person, short on faith and long on doubt. Was Thomas truly a perpetual pessimist?

Certainly, he was practical, pragmatic, cautious; but there is a great deal of evidence that suggests Thomas was not so much of an "unbeliever" as a "nonbeliever." What's the difference? The individual who is nonbelieving only wants evidence. He wants the truth. He wants an object for his faith. He or she is merely looking for rational evidence to support his or her faith. This person wants the facts, then responds to them in a positive manner.

The unbeliever, however, is often biased and prejudiced. The attitude of unbelief is that which refuses to accept any evidence no matter how well substantiated and certain.

It is the former attitude to which God always responds.

After the resurrection, Thomas was missing when Christ appeared to the disciples. When the others said, "We have seen the Lord," Thomas simply spoke for himself saying, "Unless I see the nail marks in his hands and put my finger where the nails were, and put my hand into his side, I will not believe it" (John 20:25).

A week later Jesus appeared to the disciples. The doors were locked and the curtains veiled the windows, and suddenly Jesus appeared in their midst. Then Jesus spoke directly to Thomas and said, "Put your finger here; see my hands. Reach out your hand and put it into my side. Stop doubting and believe" (John 20:27).

Nothing in the text suggests that Thomas put his hand in the nail prints of our Lord, but the text says, having been confronted with the risen Christ, he immediately cried out "My Lord and my God!" His confession was personal. That was it. The matter was settled.

Christ met Thomas at the point of his need. When an individual is honest and sincere—he or she truly wants to know—Christ will always reveal Himself to that person. Early in His ministry Christ challenged, " 'If any one chooses to do God's will, he will find out whether my teaching comes from God or whether I speak on my own' " (John 7:17). That promise is still valid today.

Christ also met Thomas at the level of his faith. He didn't reject him because of his personality or his cautious reserve. Commit as much of yourself as you can based upon what you do understand. And in time, you will find that more and more becomes apparent. That's the way faith works.

Prayer

George Mueller

This is the confidence we have in approaching God:
that if we ask anything according to his will,
he hears us.

1 John 5:14

George Mueller was educated in the universities of Germany during the period of time when rationalism was the dominant philosophy of the day. Rationalism is a humanistic philosophy that leaves God pretty much out of life, and Mueller certainly did that very thing for his first twenty years. As a young man, Mueller's life consisted of wine, women, and song. He ended up in jail, to the disgrace of his father and family, who wanted their son to become a clergyman. Mueller wanted anything but that!

At the age of twenty, while studying at the university, he was invited to the home of a friend who was a Christian. That evening Mueller was intrigued to see his friend kneel and pray—something Mueller had never seen before. At his home following the meal, the host read a chapter from the Bible—the same one that a professor of Mueller's had earlier ridiculed—and the reading of Scripture was followed by a hymn. Mueller felt so awkward that he apologized for even being there, but that night changed his life.

When he wrote his autobiography, Mueller could not remember if it was that night that he went home and knelt down for the first time to pray as he had seen his friend George Wagner do. But it is certain that Mueller was shortly thereafter converted to Jesus Christ. After his conversion, he quickly learned the secret of prayer.

In the university, Mueller had excelled as a scholar; and with the same fervent dedication, he now turned to the Scriptures and began to apply them to his life. Rejecting a rationalistic approach to life, Mueller believed that faith is believing the promises of God and then standing on them completely. At the same time, Mueller became concerned for the orphans that wandered the streets of Bristol in England. This was the beginning of the orphanages that Mueller established, which were operated on the principle of faith in God.

George Mueller never asked for money for his work, yet in response to his faith, God sent in the equivalent of more than one million U.S. dollars. When there was no food, Mueller would not allow his staff to send out an SOS for money. Instead, he would instruct, "Set the table for dinner," although there was nothing to cook, then he would go to his room and bend his knees in prayer. . .and God provided.

One of his biographers wrote that after Mueller died, it was discovered that Mueller had literally worn two depressions into the wooden floor from kneeling beside his bed in prayer.

•••

CHRIS MILBRATH

Is any one of you sick?
He should call the elders of the church to
pray over him. . . .
And the prayer offered in faith
will make the sick person well.

JAMES 5:14–15

When Chris Milbrath was working with Co-Mission in Ukraine, the last thing he ever thought would happen to him was a trip to the hospital for surgery. After all, Chris is twenty-five years of age and a handsome, healthy, strong specimen of young manhood. He's six feet five inches tall with a shock of blond hair and is endowed with the kind of good looks that turn the heads of young women.

But then unexpectedly, a stomachache didn't go away. It had to be more than indigestion. Eventually a doctor told him, "You've got a ruptured appendix, and unless you have surgery immediately, you're going to die." A second opinion was not an option.

Surgery took place the next day. It didn't go well. Infection threatened his life. A roommate who understood a little English said that he prayed and praised the Lord in his delirious stupor.

Then, halfway around the world, an older woman, a friend and supporter, suddenly woke in the middle of the night. She felt an irresistible burden to get out of bed and pray for her young friend. Later as they compared notes and made adjustment for the difference in time zones, Chris and the friend were amazed that this strange prayer burden came at the very time his life was hanging by a thread.

Within twenty-four hours, word got through to a medical missions group in Moscow that things hadn't gone well and that the hospital didn't have the resources or equipment to save his life. A small jet *just happened* to be available and was sent to airlift him to Geneva, where one of the best surgeons in Switzerland *just happened* to be available for additional surgery, which undoubtedly saved the life of this young man.

God's work—as well as His workers—is energized by prayer. The measure of our accomplishment is really the reflection of the prayer base supporting those of us who are involved in His work. Make prayer for others a vital part of your support. Your prayers make a difference. Chris Milbrath knows for sure.

• • •

PETER CAO

"You intended to harm me,
but God intended it for good to
accomplish what is now being done,
the saving of many lives."

GENESIS 50:20

If you question the fact that truth is stranger than fiction, let me tell you about Peter Cao and the uncanny set of circumstances that brought his family back together again after they were torn apart by the conflict in Vietnam. You see, when Vietnam fell,

Peter knew his future was in jeopardy. He was pastor of a church, and he also ran an orphanage filled with children whose Amerasian heritage was considered a stigma by the Vietnamese, whose racial purity had been defiled by the American soldiers.

To save his "family," Peter put five of his ten Amerasian children on military flights to the U.S. His third youngest daughter, Lehang, recalls, "When parents would decide at the last minute to remove orphans from an airlift, our father would fill the empty slots with the youngest of us."

Eventually, Peter's five children were separated from each other, their hopes dashed of ever seeing each other again. One morning, Lehang awakened at the temporary shelter where she had been placed to hear a child crying. The voice had a familiar ring to it. Could it be her little brother? Lehang says, "His face and eyes were so swollen from crying, I could not recognize him immediately. But when I looked closer and saw this boy's unusually large feet, I realized he was my two-year-old brother, Buu!"

But Lehang couldn't speak English. And try as she did, she couldn't make anyone understand that this child was her brother. Lehang tried to tell an interpreter, but the records had been mixed up, and the nickname she used for her brother was different from the official name on the documents. The next day Lehang, brokenhearted, was forced to leave and fly to another state.

When the plane arrived at its destination, the children were placed on five different buses en route to a processing center. On board each bus was a Vietnamese interpreter. As Lehang boarded the bus, she couldn't believe what she saw. Before her eyes was her elder sister, who had come on an earlier flight and was now serving as an interpreter. Soon the children were reunited.

The children prayed fervently that God would allow the whole family to be reunited—at the same time the parents were praying the same prayer. Thousands of miles of ocean and piles of government red tape separated them.

Meanwhile Peter, his wife, and five of the oldest children decided to risk everything by embarking on an old fishing boat. Before them were twenty-four grueling days at sea with nothing to eat but dry noodles and fish. For three days they went without food, and water was rationed out in a bottle cap.

Eventually, God answered prayer and the little fishing boat reached Guam. After nine months of separation, the family was reunited against almost unbelievable odds. But that's the way it almost always is when God steps in and answers prayer.

PURITY

MARY, MOTHER OF JESUS

"Blessed are you among women."

LUKE 1:42

Protestants sometimes accuse Catholics of glorifying Mary beyond the limits of what they feel is the scriptural framework, but is it possible in their attempt to glorify the Son, Protestants have ignored the handmaiden of the Lord, who was the natural mother of Jesus?

How important was her life? Her position among women from the time of Eve to the present has been unique. That alone demands that we take another look at her life and the qualities which resulted in her being the human instrument that enabled the Divine to be united with humanity.

She was a virgin and was engaged (betrothed is the King James term, which means more than engagement does today) to Joseph. But there is more, especially in relationship to women today.

Matthew traces Mary's lineage to Abraham through David,

establishing her pedigree. However, as Matthew lists the genealogy, he does something that is significant when he writes that Jacob was the father of Joseph, the husband of Mary, of whom was born Jesus, who is called Christ.

Normally, rules of grammar would have been to use a masculine pronoun when Matthew says, "Joseph the husband of Mary, of whom was born Christ," but he uses a feminine pronoun in reference to Mary to whom was born Christ. By doing this he tells us that there is no question in his mind that Mary was a virgin, not only at the time of conception, but that as Scripture says, Joseph did not have sexual relations with her until Jesus had been born.

The writers of Scripture never included details, they only gave the essentials: "God sent the angel Gabriel," writes Luke, a Syrian physician and the author of the third Gospel, "to Nazareth, a town in Galilee, to a virgin pledged to be married to a man named Joseph, a descendant of David. The virgin's name was Mary" (Luke 1:26–27).

That's how it all starts. When it became obvious that Mary was with child, "Because Joseph her husband was a righteous man and did not want to expose her to public disgrace, he had in mind to divorce her quietly," so says Matthew 1:19. After all, who would believe her story that an angel by the name of Gabriel had appeared to her? No one had ever borne a child conceived without a human father. At that point an angel appeared to Joseph, convincing him that Mary had conceived a baby from the Holy Spirit.

Take a fresh look at Mary's life. You will discover a woman of grace and beauty, with an essential, irreplaceable role in the Incarnation.

PURPOSE

PAUL KAUFFMAN

*I have no one else like him,
who takes a genuine interest in your welfare.
For everyone looks out for his own interests,
not those of Jesus Christ.*

PHILIPPIANS 2:20–21

Long ago God gave to David "men who understood the times," so that Israel would know what to do (see 1 Chronicles 12:32). Paul Kauffman, who spent most of his life in Asia, was the same kind of man. His native home was China, but when the dark specter of the Sino-Japanese War was looming on the horizon, Paul's widowed mother brought him to safer territory. His heart was always in Asia. Growing up in China, Paul spoke Chinese flawlessly, and if a Chinese heart could indwell an American body, Paul would have been the combination.

Establishing the first Chinese research center in Hong Kong in the 1960s, Paul was a man ahead of his times. In 1968, when the Bamboo Curtain was strongly protecting China from Western influence, Paul and his organization, Asian Outreach, launched a new translation of the Bible in the simplified Chinese characters Chairman Mao had insisted were necessary to teach the masses to read and write. When major publishers scoffed at the idea of publishing a new Bible for China when the country was sealed from the outside world, Kauffman set about to publish the new Bible with his own organization.

There are those who make things happen, those who watch them happen, and those who never know that anything at all is happening. For more than fifty years Paul was on the cutting edge of making things happen, and when events inside

China were reshaping the future of this massive population base, Paul interpreted them with accuracy and clarity. In the 1950s, he began disseminating information about China in a monthly newsletter; but then as the demand for information grew, the newsletter became a bimonthly publication known as the *Asian Report*.

Paul Kauffman was a type-A+ personality whose greatest legacy was his integrity and commitment to the cause of Jesus Christ. At a missions conference he once challenged people to launch something so great that it is doomed to failure unless God supernaturally steps in and undergirds the project.

Though his books are among the finest ever written, his name was not a household word to most Americans. Yet he was known to millions in Asia as a man who knew what was happening and knew how to respond to the cataclysmic events of the past fifty years.

Silenced by a devastating stroke, the last two years of his life were frustrating for a man who lived to preach, teach, and write. His seventy-seven years are now behind him, but he left behind a legacy and an example that are far more valuable than diamonds or pearls.

SACRIFICE OF LOVE

SIR ERNEST SHACKLETON

*"Greater love has no one than this,
that he lay down his life for his friends."*

JOHN 15:13

In the year 1908, the Irish explorer Sir Ernest Shackleton headed an expedition with the goal of reaching the South Pole in the Antarctic. The destination of the expedition was to cross the twenty-one hundred miles of Antarctic wasteland and reach the pole, something that had never been done before.

The fact that they were traversing uncharted wasteland locked in by ice and snow didn't deter them. En route their ship was stopped by the ice pack, crushed, and destroyed. They loaded the supplies on sleds and pursued their elusive goal.

Shackleton and his men came within ninety-seven miles of the pole and had to turn back. Those were the days when hardy men made a desperate run for it; if they succeeded, they were heroes. If they failed, they were statistics in the record book. Shackleton came closer to the pole than anyone had ever been before, but the time came when he and the men realized that to continue the expedition would result in their deaths.

They were weary and exhausted and food was running low. To continue would mean sacrificing some of the sled dogs, and with each loss, the burden of carrying equipment or even trekking would grow greater for every man. With heavy hearts, they turned and started back for the nearest outpost of civilization on South Georgia Island, some twelve hundred miles away.

Shackleton and his men had to trudge over two hundred miles of ice floes, dragging behind them a lifeboat weighing nearly a ton, taken from the ship that had brought them. When they finally reached open waters with the lifeboat, they faced an angry ocean with waves as high as ninety feet.

In his diary Shackleton told of the time when their food supplies were exhausted, save for one last ration of hardtack, a dried sort of biscuit, that was distributed to each man. Some of the men took ice or snow, melted it, and made tea while consuming their biscuit. Others, however, took the hardtack and stowed it in a food sack, thinking that they would save it for a last moment of hungry desperation.

The fire was built up, and weary, exhausted men climbed into their sleeping bags to face a restless sleep, tossing and turning.

Shackleton said that he was almost asleep when, out of the corner of his eyes, he noticed one of his most trusted men sitting up in his sleeping bag and looking about to see if anyone was watching.

Shackleton's heart sank within him as this man began to reach toward the food sack of the man next to him. This was one of his most dependable men. Never did he think that this man would steal from his neighbor. Shackleton didn't move and watched as the man took the food sack of the man next to him, opened it, and put his own hardtack in the other man's sack.

When Shackleton and the rest of the party reached their final destination seven months after they had begun, they were so hardened and emaciated that friends did not even recognize them. How did they survive? One biographer wrote, "To a man. . .those who had completed the journey reported that they felt the presence of One unseen to guide them on their perilous trek. Somehow they knew they were not alone."

God answered the prayers of these hardy explorers, for a great deal more than Irish resolve was necessary for survival. God honored the spirit of a man who was willing to give his last morsel of food to his brother. Tough men, that Shackleton and his bunch. Truly tough, as only God can make us.

TOUGH LOVE

MARY SLESSOR

"For I know the plans I have for you," declares the LORD,
"plans to prosper you and not to harm you,
plans to give you hope and a future."

JEREMIAH 29:11

Scotland of the 1840s was as barren as the nursery rhyme cupboard of Old Mother Hubbard. The decade was known as the "Hungry Forties," as crops failed and migrant workers were driven to the overcrowded, desolate cities. In 1848, Mary Mitchell Slessor was born to an alcoholic shoemaker whose wife was a weaver as well as the eventual mother of seven children. When drink finally overcame her father, the scant wages of his wife drove the family to Dundee, where young Mary grew up. At the age of eleven she was forced to work in the mill half-time. This meant schooling had to fit in with the work schedule. Home was a tiny, one-room flat with no water, no lighting, and no sanitation facilities.

It was a tough world for this redheaded, streetwise young woman. She finally dropped out of school to work in the mill, but the girl who knew how to use her knuckles with the local rowdies had a tender heart. When a missionary from the Calabar in Africa (now known as Nigeria) spoke in their local church, Mary's heart was inflamed. Everything, though, was against her becoming a missionary—everything and everybody but God. Nonetheless, God was able to use all of these circumstances in a mighty way to her advantage.

Many years later, Mary Slessor, who became known as Mary, Queen of the Calabar, wrote in her diary, "God plus one are always a majority—let me know Thou art with me." Mary Slessor—the fighting Scot from the slums of Dundee—went to an Africa that was still reeling from the horrors of the slave trade. It was diseased by such pagan customs as killing all twins because the natives were convinced that one had been fathered by the devil. Since they were uncertain as to which twin was so fathered, they immediately killed both.

The Africa to which Mary went was competing for the white man's money, weapons, and booze. The impact of Mary Slessor, who sacrificed pleasure, health, and almost her very life, is so beautifully described in a book written by James Buchan entitled *The Expendable Mary Slessor*.

Buchan describes Mary's accomplishments: "She never opposed the African ways except where they degraded the Africans themselves. She had learned from St. Paul—'Paul, laddie,' she called him—that her Lord loved these people enough to give His life for them, but loving them never meant acquiescing to the base aspects of pagan culture. She threatened and begged in order to save lives; she saved the lives of many babies destined to die in the bush, adopting some of them as her own children. She fought for the right of the African women to be free from death at the whim of a man. For nearly forty years—until her death in 1915—she lived as an African, often in a village hut. When she died, thousands of Africans wept for the Eka Kpukpro Owo—'Mother of all the peoples.'"

One of the great Christian leaders of the last century—Mary Slessor, Queen of the Calabar.

TRUST

GO PUAN SENG

Trust in the LORD with all your heart and
lean not on your own understanding;
in all your ways acknowledge him,
and he will make your paths straight.

PROVERBS 3:5–6

In his book *Refuge and Strength*, Go Puan Seng tells of the four years during World War II when he and his family were only one step from death as they eluded the Japanese soldiers in the jungles of the Philippines. When United Press International reviewed the book, they pointed out that the purpose of Seng's book is to remind the world that absolute and complete faith in

God and in the promises of His Word is sufficient to take one through the most serious crisis.

When World War II broke out, Seng was the publisher of the influential Chinese newspaper based in Manila called the *Fukien Times*. When the swords began to rattle, Seng came out strongly against the Japanese for their aggression in the Philippines. Seng strongly urged resistance. When Manila fell in December 1941, Go Puan Seng found himself a hunted man, with his name on the list of most wanted men.

The days of his fiery editorials and rhetoric against the invaders were over, and Jimmy Go, as he was known to his friends, began to live one day at a time. In spite of the constant danger to his life, God gave Seng a quiet confidence that He would guide and protect him.

Shortly after Seng took his family and escaped to the mountainous jungles some thirty miles from Manila, the former publisher found himself at the point of despair, and in desperation, he cried out to God. In the stillness of the jungle, God met him! And from that point on, Jimmy Go was never in total despair. At times God led them through the enemy lines, as they prayed fervently that God would spare their lives. And, in response to their prayers, the soldiers would wave them on, not realizing that one of the enemy's most wanted men was in the horse-drawn cart.

It was through the Word of God that specific guidance was given to the party in exile, guidance at times that seemed totally out of keeping with the circumstances. In his own words, Go tells of an instance when "We were surrounded inside the Japanese General Yamashita's battle lines. That was in 1944 (about the end of December), when the retreating Japanese soldiers were pouring into our mountains from the west side. By all human instincts, we should go east, run deeper into the mountains to keep distance between us and the retreating Japanese soldiers. We prayed to God, and God's answer was in the good Book of Joshua. It said, 'Goeth down westward to the coast. . . .' When

I told my group that we were going westward, many of them were against me. Some of them left me. Ten of them went east instead of westward. They never have returned. . . . We went westward. We did encounter Japanese soldiers retreating from the front lines, but they did not do us any harm."

When a man has found that God is our refuge and our strength, nothing else really matters but that He guides and leads us hour by hour.

• • •

J. C. PENNEY

"I am the resurrection and the life.
He who believes in me will live,
even though he dies;
and whoever lives and believes in me will never die."

JOHN 11:25–26

When the U. S. stock market crashed in 1929, J. C. Penney had made some unwise personal commitments. He became so worried that he could not sleep. Night after night, Penney tossed and turned and became obsessed with a fear of death. Out of this nervous condition, he developed a disease known as shingles. He was hospitalized and given sedation to relieve the intense pain. A combination of circumstances, physical and mental, led him to believe he would not live until morning. He wrote farewell letters to his wife and son. He sincerely believed that the monster of death was lurking for him in the hospital corridors.

Somehow, Penney lived through the night. The next morning the fear-torn Penney heard a group of people singing in the hospital chapel. The words of the song drifted down the halls: "God Will Take Care of You." He listened to the words intently.

They were followed by a reading of a Scripture passage and prayer.

Then, something happened. In Penney's own words: "I can't explain it. I can only call it a miracle. I felt as if I had been instantly lifted out of the darkness of a dungeon into warm, brilliant sunlight. I felt as if I had been transported from hell to paradise. I felt the power of God as I had never felt it before. . . . From that day to this, my life has been free from worry."

Penney's fear of death was suddenly cut down to size. Neither Penney nor anyone else could explain it by reason; yet countless millions have discovered that when they committed their lives to Christ, they found the reality of a supernatural peace that cuts the fear of death down to proper size.

Simple faith in God goes beyond reason, yet it gives peace that is most reasonable. What more beautiful expression of peace in the face of death is there than the Twenty-third Psalm (KJV): "The LORD is my shepherd; I shall not want. . . . Yea, though I walk through the valley of the shadow of death, I will fear no evil: for thou art with me."

Christian faith is unique in its assertion that the grave is not the end but merely the beginning of an eternal tomorrow. How beautiful are the words of Christ: " 'I am the resurrection and the life. He who believes in me will live, even though he dies; and whoever lives and believes in me will never die' " (John 11:25–26).

• • •

HEZEKIAH

The LORD is good, a strong hold in the day of trouble.

NAHUM 1:7 KJV

If ever a man had reason to feel that God had let him down, that man was Hezekiah, the king of Judah who ascended the throne of David about 726 B.C.

Having replaced his father, Ahaz, who had been a careless ruler, Hezekiah began a great reformation. He broke down the idols Ahaz had set up. He reopened the temple and restored the service of God. He even used his own funds to provide for restoration and repairs.

In the sixth year of Hezekiah's reign, the Northern Kingdom (Israel) fell to Sennacherib, king of Assyria. True, Israel was often an enemy of Judah, but they were all related by blood through King David, who had established the kingdom. So when Assyria wiped out Israel, Hezekiah knew that his borders were more vulnerable.

Then Sennacherib moved against Judah. Here's the text: "After all that Hezekiah had so faithfully done, Sennacherib king of Assyria came and invaded Judah!" If Hezekiah felt God had let him down or that God owed him better treatment, he didn't say so. Why? Hezekiah had faced the enemy more than once and had learned that what counts isn't the strength of your enemy but the strength of your defense, and he had learned God can be that defense.

You will find the whole text in the Old Testament, in 2 Chronicles 32. In Hezekiah's response there are two very important guidelines that will help you no matter who or what has come to invade your private world. First, Hezekiah did what he could do himself. He built walls supporting the walls that were already there. He made weapons; he encouraged the men in the army by reminding them that with Sennacherib was only the arm of flesh, but with them was the "Lord our God to help them and to fight their battles."

Hezekiah didn't stop there. The second approach was this: "King Hezekiah and the prophet Isaiah. . .cried out in prayer to heaven about this" (2 Chronicles 32:20). The government and the religious community united their hearts in fervent prayer.

They didn't talk about prayer. They prayed! And God gave tremendous deliverance.

Learn from Hezekiah. Confront problems by doing what you can yourself. Encourage others to join you, to stand together, and then seek God with all your heart. The same God who gave deliverance to Hezekiah is still giving deliverance.

WISDOM

JOHN THE BAPTIST

"John. . .will be great in the sight of the Lord."

LUKE 1:13, 15

One of the evidences for the supernatural character of the Bible is the manner in which the flaws of heroes are portrayed. The writers never gloss over their faults or omit their failures as we tend to do of ourselves. In unvarnished strokes the writers of Scripture describe people just as they are. Subsequently, a vast army of men and women march across the stage of redemption fully human, completely real. Such was the man who served as the forerunner of Jesus, a man described as "John the Baptist," a name given to him based on his desire to seal repentance with baptism so that all would know of the change of heart people had experienced.

Had John walked into a local church today, he probably would be asked to leave, or, at best, sit in the overflow area where more air circulated. John was totally unconventional. Dressed in camel's hair, he had the appearance of a social misfit. His hair was wild and his beard unkempt. His skin was leathery and tough. His eyes, bright and penetrating.

When someone asked Jesus about John's appearance, He

replied, " 'What did you go out into the desert to see? A reed swayed by the wind? If not, what did you go out to see? A man dressed in fine clothes? No, those who wear fine clothes are in kings' palaces' " (Matthew 11:7–8). John's diet was unconventional as well. Locusts and wild honey were his staples, according to local reports.

John's character was also unconventional. A man's man with a heart after God, John's character was without flaw. When the crowds came to hear him speak, instead of basking in the glory of notoriety, John made it clear that he was only the forerunner, the front man of the coming Messiah. Is it any wonder that Jesus said of him, " 'Among those born of women there has not risen anyone greater than John the Baptist' " (Matthew 11:11)? It was this man whom Jesus sought out when He began His ministry and asked to be baptized in water, thereby giving us an example that we ought to follow.

Yet with his rugged character and integrity, John was fully human. When he was thrown into prison as the result of making political enemies, he sent his disciples to Jesus asking, " 'Are you the one who was to come, or should we expect someone else?' " (Matthew 11:3).

John was also unconventional in his message. He never pitched his message to the grandstand. He openly and even defiantly proclaimed the truth in spite of the fact that prison and death resulted.

John's life speaks clearly to the flaws of our culture today. His example tells us that those who really walk with God will be out of touch with the mind-set and mentality of our age. This isn't to suggest that we adopt weird, strange dress and think that we are godly, but it does imply we should proclaim loudly and clearly that those who walk the narrow pathway will always have plenty of elbow room.

Long before John, God spoke to Samuel, " 'The LORD does not look at the things man looks at. Man looks at the outward appearance, but the LORD looks at the heart' " (1 Samuel 16:7).

···

A. W. TOZER

Since we have these promises,
dear friends, let us purify ourselves
from everything that contaminates body and spirit.

2 CORINTHIANS 7:1

On his tombstone there is a simple epitaph that reads, "A. W. Tozer—A Man of God." That's it. He was born on April 21, 1897, and at the age of seventeen was converted to faith in Jesus Christ. Shortly thereafter, he cleaned out a corner in the basement of his father's home and began to saturate himself in the book that became his master, the Bible.

Aiden Wilson Tozer, or A. W. as he preferred, using only the initials of his name, never got a formal seminary education. He was basically a self-taught student of the Book, yet his writings touched a generation for God. The books that Tozer wrote are not for shallow searchers looking for the "quick fix" or an "instant solution" to a problem that leaves you feeling good. Reading Tozer demands concentration, taking what he says in "bite sizes," allowing the reader to digest what he says and understand God in a new way.

Tozer brings you into direct confrontation with the Almighty, and when you close one of his books, you know that you have confronted the claims of Scripture in a new way, one which demands a decision. Two of his books, *The Pursuit of God* and *The Knowledge of the Holy,* have become classics, a tremendous achievement for a man who never received formal theological education. Leonard Ravenhill once spoke of Tozer saying, "I fear that we shall never see another Tozer. Men like him are not college bred but Spirit taught." He was right.

In one of his books Tozer wrote, "God discovers Himself

to babes, and hides Himself in thick darkness from the wise and the prudent. We must simplify our approach to Him. We must strip down to essentials, and they will be found to be blessedly few."

Tozer described himself as a mystic, a term that conjures up images of someone who walks about with his head in a cloud, not quite in touch with reality. Writing about Tozer, Warren Wiersbe says that Tozer's mysticism was different. He defines it saying, "A mystic is simply a person who: 1) sees a real spiritual world beyond the world of sense; 2) seeks to please God rather than the crowd; 3) cultivates a close fellowship with God, senses His presence everywhere; and 4) relates his experience to the practical things of life."

Tozer believed that a lot of people know a great deal *about* God—they know the language, the songs, and the culture—but they do not know God Himself. They have been taught about God, but not taught by God, and there is a difference.

Most of Tozer's books were an outgrowth of messages he preached, and they uniformly brought hearers into direct confrontation with God. He would ask, "Is God real to you?" "Is your heart hungering and thirsting after personal righteousness?" "Is yours a firsthand experience with Him, or a secondhand one through others?"

He never owned an automobile, and even after he became a successful author and public speaker, he was never affected by his money. To the contrary, he gave most of his money away to those who were hurting and in need. Some considered him strange, and his views on music and entertainment were out of step with his generation, but he walked in step with the Holy Spirit and gave us a legacy of holiness and truth. A. W. Tozer—a man of God as his tombstone truthfully asserts.

...

MATTHEW MAURY

You made him ruler over the works of your hands;
you put everything under his feet.

PSALM 8:6

Some of the greatest scientific discoveries of all time were made
by men who not only believed the Bible but followed its insights.
Such was the naval commander Matthew Maury, whose research
and charts pioneered the field of oceanography and navigation.

It started almost a century and a half ago, when Maury sustained a leg injury that left him bedridden. Maury was a sailor
who had been around the world a couple of times. However, in
1839, while he was recovering from the injury, his wife read the
Bible to him.

One day Mrs. Maury was reading Psalm 8, which talks
about God's creative power and might. The words seemed to
ignite her husband's imagination and thinking. These are the
words that spoke so loudly: "You [meaning God] have made
him [that's humanity] to have dominion over the works of Your
hands; You have put all things under his feet [that's man's
authority], all sheep and oxen, even the beasts of the field, the
birds of the air, and the fish of the sea, that pass through the
paths of the seas" (Psalm 8:6–8 NKJV).

Maury began thinking, "How can the sea have paths?" Then
he began thinking that if he ever got back to the sea, he would
do research on the paths of the sea. Two years later Maury went
back to the navy and was put in charge of their depot of charts
and instruments. In this post, he launched an investigation of the
ocean currents, which kept him busy for the next twenty years
and won him the title "Pathfinder of the Seas."

He designated logbooks and gave them to sea captains

from many nations. He asked them to keep a daily record of their location, wind speed, and weather conditions. He persuaded sailors to drop bottles in the sea with messages recording the date and location.

Eventually Commander Maury was responsible for charting the Gulf Stream and the Labrador Stream and laid the foundation for the U.S. Naval Observatory. Maury's work cut precious days from travel time as captains took advantage of the natural currents of the sea. His discoveries saved countless lives by helping navigators avoid dangerous storms at sea. And all of this resulted from the discoveries of a man who believed that the phrase "the paths of the seas" was not poetic license the psalmist took three thousand years ago but was an accurate statement science had not quite caught up with yet.

Life ceases to be a riddle when you gain God's perspective, and that is the secret of the Bible.

A FEW
FINAL THOUGHTS

In the pages of this book, we have profiled people who have made a difference in our world, common ordinary people with an extraordinary purpose in life.

You probably noticed a pattern. In the lives of many of the people profiled, there was a spiritual encounter with God through His Son, Jesus Christ. Though they may have described it in different terms, it was the same experience had by Nicodemus, a religious leader who came to Jesus by night. Jesus told him simply that he needed to be born again. "Except a man be born again," said Jesus, "he cannot see the kingdom of God" (John 3:3 KJV).

This personal encounter with Jesus Christ—whether it was

the unusual kind of encounter that Saul of Tarsus had on the road to Damascus or the slow, gradual understanding of who Jesus is and what He did, whereby someone embraces Him as Lord and Savior—is what gave so many of my heroes direction and purpose for their lives. And when they found Him, their goals changed with a redirected focus in life.

Having stressed that real purpose in life comes through a personal relationship with Jesus Christ, by way of contrast, let's focus on the lives of a few other people who were rich and famous and by virtue of their attainment, beauty, or fame were considered to be heroes in their day.

George Eastman's goal in life was financial success. He reached it, too. In camera shops the world over, you will find the yellow boxes of film made by the Eastman Kodak Company. But reaching his goal didn't satisfy him. One morning he conferred with his business associates, then went to his room and scribbled these words on a piece of paper: "My work is finished. Why wait?" He then took a German Luger semiautomatic, put it to his head, and ended his life in suicide.

If fame or beauty is your goal in life, consider Marilyn Monroe. This gifted and beautiful woman overdosed on Nebutol—a drug that stopped her heart. My hometown newspaper editorialized, "Marilyn Monroe died Sunday proving that even $10,000 a week won't buy peace of mind."

If accomplishment in life is your goal, consider Ernest Hemingway. He won the Nobel Prize for literature and was famous for his pungent character descriptions in works like *A Farewell to Arms, The Old Man and the Sea,* and *For Whom the Bell Tolls.* Hemingway fatally shot himself in the head with a 12-gauge shotgun. Obviously, a person can be tremendously talented and yet unfulfilled and miserable.

In 1923, a group of men who were considered winners met at the Edgewater Beach Hotel in Chicago. Present were some of the world's most successful financiers: Charles Schwab, president of Bethlehem Steel; Samuel Insull, the president of the world's largest utility company; Richard Whitney, the president of the New York Stock Exchange; Albert Fall, then a member of the U.S. president's cabinet; as well as Jesse Livermore, Ivan Kruger, and Leon Frazer, heads of the world's largest investment firm, the greatest monopoly in the world, and the Bank of International Settlement, respectively.

Charles Schwab died bankrupt and lived on borrowed money for the last five years of his life. Samuel Insull ended his days as a fugitive, broke, and living in a foreign country. Richard Whitney was released from Sing Sing prison to die at home. Albert Fall was pardoned so that he also could die at home. The last three mentioned—Jesse Livermore, Ivan Kruger, and Leon Frazer—all died as suicides.

These individuals made it to the top. They had the world at their feet; but once they reached their goals, something went wrong. Plenty wrong.

For a few moments, focus your attention on these individuals, people also considered to be winners: Viscount Castlereaugh, the British foreign secretary; Lee Ki Poong, vice president of Korea; Edwin Armstrong, who invented FM radio; Arthur Chevrolet, the designer of the automobile built by General Motors; Lester Hunt, governor of the state of Wyoming; and James Forrestal, the American secretary of state. And to this group I could add the names of Ernest Hemingway, Marilyn Monroe, and Kurt Cobain for a beginning. What do they have in common? Two things: They were successful and they were also suicidal.

If reaching the top is success, they made it; but as Dr. Charles Malik, the Lebanese statesman and former president of the U.N. General Assembly defined success, they fell dismally short. "Success," said Malik, "is seeking and knowing and loving and obeying God; and if you seek, you will know; and if you know, you will love; and if you love, you will obey."

Success from God's point of view, from the vantage of looking back over life and valuing relationships, is vastly different. Jesus put it, " 'What good is it for a man to gain the whole world, yet forfeit his soul? Or what can a man give in exchange for his soul?' " (Mark 8:36–37).

If a relationship with God has been missing in your life, right now pray a simple prayer something like this: "Father, I believe You sent Your Son into the world to make a difference in my life. I do believe that He lived, died, and rose again. I not only want Him to forgive me of my sins, but I want Him to be my Lord and Savior. Lord, Jesus, please take over my life and give me a purpose in living."

Then I hope you will write to me and let me know what happens. I'll be glad to answer your questions.

With God's help you can make your life count for something lasting and worthwhile, something that will endure the fire. You, too, can be a person who makes a difference in our world.

REFERENCE NOTES

i Kitty Muggeridge, "Mother Teresa," *Eternity,* December 1983, p. 101.

ii Lori Sharn, "Mother Teresa's Heart Never Left the Poor," *U.S.A. Today,* September 8, 1997, p. 17A.

iii Diego Ribadeneira and Indira Lakshmanan, *Seattle Post-Intelligencer,* "Mother Teresa," Sept. 6, 1997, p. 1.

iv Bruce Shelley, *Church History in Plain Language* (Chicago: Word, 1982), p. 119.

v Billy Graham, *Just As I Am* (San Francisco: HarperCollins Zondervan, 1997), p. 24.

vi Eliot Wirt Sherwood, *Billy* (Wheaton, Ill.: Crossway Books, 1997), p. 20.

vii J. C. Pollock, *Hudson Taylor and Maria* (New York: McGraw-Hill, 1962), pp. 15, 16.

viii Ruth Tucker, *From Jerusalem to Irian Jaya* (Grand Rapids: Zondervan, 1983), p. 176.

ix From "The Acts of Paul and Thecla," as quoted by *Christianity Today,* August 11, 1997, p. 39.

x William R. Moody, *The Life of Dwight L. Moody* (New York: Fleming H. Revell, 1900), p. 402.

xi *Moody,* p. 403.